*To Jerry
with God's
Blessings*

*Fr. Roy Lopez
10/19/04*

EL POCHE

Memoirs of a Mexican American Padre

EL POCHE

Memoirs of a Mexican American Padre

FATHER SEVERINO LOPEZ,
C.M.F.

CLARETIAN PUBLICATIONS
Chicago, Illinois

El Poche: Memoirs of a Mexican American Padre

© 2004 by Severino Lopez, C.M.F.

All rights reserved. No parts of this book may be used or reproduced in any form without permission from the publisher:

>   Claretian Publications
>   205 W. Monroe Street
>   Chicago, IL 60606
>   312-236-7782
>   www.claretianpubs.org

International Standard Book Number (ISBN) 0-89570-501-X
Cover design by Tom A. Wright.
Cover photo by Martin Lueders.

Unless otherwise noted, photos in this book appear courtesy of the Claretian Archives, Chicago, and Father Severino Lopez. C.M.F.
Printed and bound in the United States of America,

Contents

Foreword
9

Introduction: El Poche
13

Roots: Don Severino and Mexico (1888-1915)
15

Move to California (1915-1919)
18

Off to Illinois (1919-1925)
24

Into the city: Chicago (1926-1932)
28

California seminary (1932-1944)
36

Ordination (1944)
54

Beginning of ministry (1944-1946)
57

California and Texas (1946-1953)
70

Back to Chicago (1953-1963)
76

To Mexico and back (1963-1972)
83

Shifting around (1972-1974)
86

Dark night of the soul (1974-1977)
90

Back on track (1977-1984)
97

A touch of mission work and Casa Claret (1984-1990)
101

Finally, sabbatical (1990)
112

Back in the saddle, heading south (1991-2001)
114

Lending a hand (since 2001)
124

Conclusion
131

Foreword

When I celebrated my 70th birthday a few years back, one of the gifts I received was a little booklet that recorded all the significant events of July 29, 1932 (my birthday). But I noticed it left out one important happening that was going to have an effect on many lives over 60 years to come: A young Mexican lad from Chicago's South Side entered the minor seminary to begin 12 years of preparation for the priesthood with the Claretian Missionaries, a ministry that would extend from 1944 to 2004 and beyond. It was Severino Lopez.

For much of those 60 years my life has been intertwined with Father Sevy in many ways. We first made acquaintance sometime in the early 1950s, and our paths have crossed and merged many times since. For the last 12 years, Father Sevy has served as parochial vicar of Corpus Christi Parish in Stone Mountain, Georgia, where I have served as its pastor for that same length of time.

Probably the most common remark made about Father

Sevy's life and work is, "Isn't he amazing?" It's one thing to still be doing some work at age 86, but it's quite another to be living a fully active life as a priest, giving homilies that sometimes border on great, engaging in lively exchanges with others about politics and social justice, fighting for the rights of the underprivileged, and even playing golf!

Some years ago the noted Jesuit priest, Father John LaFarge, was giving a lecture at the Catholic University of America in Washington, D.C. During the question and answer session, a priest began, "Father, I'm just an ordinary parish priest..." And LaFarge broke in, "Just a minute, Father. There is no such thing as an 'ordinary' parish priest. Every parish priest is extraordinary."

That thought kept coming to mind as I penned these few lines of introduction. There's a lot of truth in it, and it is even truer of the priest who strives to combine being a parish priest with living in community life as a religious.

Some of the stories Sevy relates will make you laugh, others might make you cringe. My favorite one is about the time Sevy and his buddies were punished for riding a neighbor's horses without permission. Sevy had not even been at the scene of the crime, but his superior at the seminary reasoned, "If he had been with his friends, he would have been riding, too!"

There are stories that show how religious life often seemed incompatible with a healthy human way of living. The rigidity of seminary discipline showed its Jansenist roots, as outlined in the small book of rules titled *The Mirror*. Touching in any form was forbidden, and consequently contact sports were not allowed, nor were so-called "particular friendships." This was an effort to avoid familiarity, but it served as a way of thwarting human development through warm friendships. The seminarians were only able to form human relationships on a superficial level. Sevy speaks also of racial prejudice, which probably stemmed from immigrant superiors wanting to gain acceptance for themselves and their congregation in American society. But much like the sexual abuse scandal that has come to light in the church today, the consequences are long-lasting. Racial prejudice had lasting effects on Sevy's development and no doubt on that of many others.

But what I think is much more important in these memoirs is the fact that when we share our stories with one another we come to a greater respect for each other. There's a strong lesson here for both the religious life and life in general. Many times we stand in judgment of someone precisely because we don't know his or her story. When we see the events and feelings and experiences that have come together to form a particular life, it gives us a whole new perspective on why and how a person acts in any given situation and how we should respond to that person.

It shows us, too, that no matter what the circumstances life deals to us, we are able to rise above them and make something good of our life for ourselves and for others. Sevy describes his dark night of the soul, when he momentarily doubted his vocation to the priesthood. A fear among many of us priests at that time was that all the good priests were leaving. One day I expressed this fear to a wonderful layman, Robert Burns, who spent many years as my coworker in Claretian ministries. He looked at me and said, "The contrary is true; The good ones are staying. The ones that stay are those who have faith."

This is not to imply that the many good men who left did

not have faith, but rather that the faith of those who stayed was being tested in a special way. And Sevy's response to that test of faith made him victor over his dark night. And faith is what made it possible for El Poche to live up to Longfellow's prediction in the "Psalm of Life" that he quotes in the beginning of this book: "We *can* make our lives sublime."

—*Father Greg Kenny, C.M.F.*

Introduction: El Poche

As a youngster in Mexico, I was given the nickname "El Poche." The word *pocho* in Spanish actually means faded or underdeveloped. The term *el poche*, derived from *pocho*, was popular during the early California days when the state seceded from Mexico and became part of the United States. The expression applied to people whose lives were shaped by two different cultures—Mexican and American. Evidently, it suited me since I had been born in California and of Mexican parents. The cultural intermingling showed in a person's speech and lifestyle. The term *el poche* eventually took on a mild but still disparaging tone characterizing an ambivalent, awkward person lost in the decision making process.

In writing these memoirs I often refer to "el poche syndrome," moments of my life when I had doubts, became confused, or experienced a dark night of the soul. However, God in his goodness made me realize that I was a full-fledged child of his and that the path he called me to follow was the one I was on.

I have decided to share my story and hope that those who may at times feel doubt will benefit from reading my memoirs. Henry Wadsworth Longfellow, an American poet of the 19th century, expressed a similar thought in his poem "A Psalm of Life."

> *Lives of great men all remind us,*
> *We can make our lives sublime*
> *And, departing, leave behind us,*
> *Footprints on the sands of time.*
> *Footprints that perhaps another,*
> *Sailing o'er life's solemn main,*
> *A forlorn and shipwrecked brother,*
> *Seeing, shall take heart again.*

Roots: Don Severino and Mexico

1888-1915

To the average American, Mexico is simply the country "south of the border." Many others look at it simply as a springboard for all those "illegals" in our country. As Mexico's former ambassador to the United Nations, Adolfo Aguilar Sinze, once told the *New York Times*, "The U.S. considers our country its own backyard." While U.S. tourists vacationing at Mexican beaches, hotels, and the many places of interest look upon Mexico as a "good deal," few Americans know the history of this beautiful country.

As a Mexican American, I have always followed and preserved my interest in Mexico. I agonized as I witnessed the failure of the North American Free Trade Agreement, a failure predicted by many of my constituents. I looked at President Vicente Fox's election as a happy day for Mexico's future but was sadly disappointed years later as I witnessed Fox's efforts being thwarted by a divided legislature and the poor economy in the United States. I am once again encouraged, though, by the proposal recently renewed by Robert Pastor, director of the Center of North American Studies at American University in Washington, D.C. The proposal was originally made by Fox, and Pastor agrees: "You cannot have a community unless you lift the poorest up."

Pastor proposes that the three NAFTA partners, for the good of all, establish a European Union-style infrastructure fund of $200 billion over a 10-year period. This investment, he says, would yield more return for the U.S. economy than any other in history. This investment would also strengthen the economy of Mexico, the top purchaser of American goods, and would also reduce the need for illegal immigration. This type of fund would also allow for systems of telecommunication, construction of better highways, more technical education, and increased opportunities for skilled workers, especially rural areas, to have a better quality of life. It is a dream, perhaps, but I pray for that.

As I observe Mexico's struggle to occupy its rightful place among the nations of the world, I wistfully reflect back on history. There was a time when this country enjoyed a relative peace and prosperity during the reign of Porfirio Diaz, a benevolent dictator. Is that an oxymoron? Perhaps. How can peace and prosperity coexist in a dictatorship?

After two futile attempts at the presidency, Diaz was finally elected in 1884, at 50 years of age. His administration was characterized by a period of stability and a strong economy. The mining industry had boomed which required manufacturing plants, larger corporate investments, and foreign trade. More people had jobs, and income from the government contracts exceeded expenditure. Economic prosperity progressed. There was a marked interest in education throughout the land as schools and colleges improved. This gave rise to middle class intellectuals and professionals.

My father, Don Severino, was a beneficiary of this noticeable surge in the late Porfirian era. He was born in Las Cruces, Jalisco, on February 11, 1888 and eventually moved to La Piedad, Michoacan—a city of approximately 50,000 people—to take advantage of better opportunities for education. From his early years, Don Severino enjoyed his studies. His quest for knowledge and truth led him to join a group of young intellectuals who would gather locally to discuss the classics. For their pastime, they would entertain *el pueblo* with dramatic performances and *declamaciónes*, a combination of poetic and patriotic deliveries. A priest from the local parish and a prominent layperson would be the counselor or animator of such groups. This format was then developed and established in other towns and cities as an activity for young people. It developed into the Acción Catolica de Juventud Mexicana (ACJM), which was effective prior, during, and after the persecution of the Catholic Church by the government during the years 1925 to 1930.

Severino was active with this group until his marriage in 1910 to a woman named Melania. Sadly, she and their firstborn child died in the following year, causing a tremendous gloom in his life. Eventually he met Isabel Parra, who was the daughter of a landowner and who recently had moved from Guanajuato to Degollado. Severino had moved to La Piedad, but would periodically cover the distance of eight miles between Degollado and La Piedad in order to see *la huera*, a term of endearment he used in reference to Isabel's light complexion. They eventually married in June 1912.

Move to California

1915-1919

By 1910 the Mexican Revolution was in full swing. Within the next few years, Mexico witnessed the ouster of Diaz by Francisco Madero, who was then murdered by General Victoriano Huerta, who then declared himself dictator. Huerta was shortly pushed out of power, too, and another revolutionary assumed power. This national upheaval profoundly affected Severino, and on December 1915 he decided to leave Mexico temporarily until this unrest had settled down. With his wife, Isabel (Chabela), and their two children, Roberto and Carlota, they fled to California.

He arrived at Azusa, California where his compadre, Jesús Ayala, offered him lodging. That area of California did not offer the opportunities that Severino sought as a journalist, so he decided to seek other avenues of work for survival. Word got around that some silver mines had become active, and were hiring men in the area of California's Eastern Sierra, adjacent to the town of Lone Pine.

Years prior, this area had become well known for its silver

mines, which in the past, according to mine boom writers, had produced $28 million in rich ore. My father decided to venture this new experience, and the family headed for Owens Valley, a small settlement south of Lone Pine on the shore of Lake Owens. They settled in a town called Keeler. Decades earlier, a stream of immigration brought settlers there and it was predicted that in a not too distant future Owens Valley would become the most densely populated area of the Eastern Sierra Mountains. Its fertile land was fit for agriculture and a large section of it was ideal for pleasure seekers since it abounded in game, fish, and natural beauty.

This would not be for long, though, as the area had begun to experience desolation brought about by the diversion of water toward Los Angeles in addition to the building of the Mulholland Project—a saga recorded in the annals of California history. Years later, Will Rogers, a well-known humorist, had this to say about Owens Valley:

Ten years ago this was a wonderful valley, with one quarter of a million acres of healthy fruit and alfalfa crops. But Los Angeles required more water for the Chamber of Commerce to drink toasts to its growth, more water to dilute its orange juice, and more water for its geraniums to delight the tourists, while the giant cottonwoods all died. Only a valley of desolation remains.
                      (*The Story of Inyo* by W.A. Chalfant, 1933)

When the Lopez family settled in Keeler, Owens Lake was no longer navigable. In earlier years a little steamer, "The Bessie Brady," had been launched to help move silver bullion from the Cerro Gordo mine. It made a daily round trip starting three miles north of Keeler, where a wharf was built, to Cartago across the lake. This mode of transportation ceased as the Cerro Gordo Mine reduced its operation. Ground transportation in the area was encouraged as the production of salt, soda, and borax took on greater importance. Mule teams were being used to transport these products taken from the waters of Lake Owens.

Upon arriving at Keeler and the Owens Lake area, Severino discovered mining activity in the area had not increased to a large extent, and he believed the promise of mining jobs was just a ruse to attract much-needed workers for the production of borax and soda. But there was no alternative for Severino but to remain and support his family through the availability of local employment. The film industry had begun to hire extras for silent movies being produced in the outskirts of Lone Pine, and Severino was attracted to the companies on location, but his lack of proficiency in English proved to be a drawback.

The story of my life begins on the evening of September 9, 1918 when Rafael Parra, Isabel's brother who had come to live with them, met Severino at the door as he returned from work. "Isabel is having a child," he said nervously. Two of Severino's other children were born at home in Mexico, and in both cases Isabel was assisted by a mid-wife. So Severino alerted Victoria Hoyos, who had assisted other women with childbirth, to come immediately. She was the wife of his compadre, Manuel Hoyos. Manuel and Victoria had come from Michoacan years earlier and had assisted the Lopez family as they settled in Keeler.

Victoria, of course, responded to Severino's urgent request and assisted Isabel in giving birth to her third child—a boy. The following day, Severino went to Lone Pine and visited the mission church that had recently been built at the request of the archbishop from Los Angeles. Severino was told that there was no resident priest and that none would be available for about three months.

When I was in the seminary I needed to obtain a copy of my baptismal certificate, and it was only then that I discovered I had not been baptized until March 1919 at Santa Rosa in Lone Pine—more than six months after my birth. Knowing how devout both of my parents were, I was a bit surprised and on one occasion asked my mother why they waited so long for my christening. *No habia cura*, was her reply—"There was no priest available."

Years later the book *The Desert Padre*, by Joan Brooks, fell into my hands. It tells the story of Father John J. Crowley, who worked in the County of Inyo from 1919 to 1940. At that time, this part of California was still under the jurisdiction of the Archdiocese of Los Angeles. Father Crowley's Parish included Death Valley to the east, Mono Lake to the north, Mt. Whitney area to the west, and Kern County to the south. Crowley's words made it clear why it took six months for me to be baptized at Santa Rosa:

> *With such an expanse of territory it was out of the question to establish a headquarters, and I thus gained the enviable reputation of being an "ecclesiastical" tramp covering over 50,000 miles, or twice around the globe, in 14 months.*

I was christened Severino, after my father. I really do not know much as to what transpired in Keeler during the days and months following my birth. Borrowing a few facts from

The Desert Padre, I see that Keeler had grown to be a cute little community supported by the small mining activities that continued in the area, but was supported mainly by the soda-borax plant in the neighborhood. It provided employment for a large portion of Mexican men who lived nearby with their families. The Catholic Extension Society in Chicago provided a substantial fund that helped toward the building of a chapel and catechist center. In the settlement, during his leisure hours and especially on weekends, my father would assist the catechists at the center to promote activities among Mexican Catholics, since the visits of a priest to Keeler were less frequent.

Meanwhile, the unsettled political situation in Mexico that prompted Severino to leave with his family and find shelter in the U.S. was getting worse. The following facts have been gleaned from Alan Riding's book *The Distant Neighbors: A Portrait of the Mexicans* (Knopf, 1985):

> *Huerta, who took over the presidency, gave in to Venustiano Carranza, Governor of Coahuila, a state in northern Mexico. He in turn formed his own army, and with the help of Alvaro Obregon and Plutarco Elias Calles, he began to move south toward Mexico City. Pancho Villa, who was beginning his activities in Torreon, also pledged his loyalty to Carranza. He formed his own army as well, and began advancing through Central Mexico.*
>
> *Pancho Villa attracted the worst possible element. They were normally given a free hand as they robbed and plundered Villages along their way. One of these euphemistically called "generals" of Pancho Villa was Inez Chavez. He had acquired a reputa-*

tion of being cruel and senseless, and was more of a bandido *than a general.*

Off to Illinois
1919-1925

Don Marcelo Parra, my maternal grandfather, had moved from La Piedad, Michoacan to Degollado, where he had bought a farm on the outskirts of the town. He remarried after his wife's death and built a home within the town. His eldest daughter Josefa had remained single and stayed with him taking care of the home and the young children from the second wife. She was known throughout the town as a charitable person, instructing other children and preparing them for the sacraments. She was a member of the parish sodality and very devoted to the Holy Eucharist. She attended Mass and received Communion as often as her busy life would permit.

General Inez Chavez decided to enter Degollado and plunder the town, as he had done other villages. The residents had been forewarned and were prepared to resist. On Dec. 24, 1917 (when my mother was pregnant with me), Inez Chavez attempted to take Degollado by surprise, but he was repelled. The men in the town were well armed and held him at bay hoping a group from the neighboring town of Yurecuaro would come to their aid. But Chavez broke through, captured the town, executed its leaders, and set fire to many buildings.

While Marcelo Parra was away from his home, the soldiers broke in. Upon seeing Josefa and Coletta Melendez, *una criada*, or maid, who was assisting with the housework, they dragged them out of the house. The soldiers decided to take them to the barracks so the men could satisfy their lust. But as the group proceeded along the street, Josefa and Coletta broke from their grasp, and after spotting a burning building decided it was better to be consumed by flames than accede to the prurient desires of their captors.

Word of this heroic act eventually spread through the town. Josefa and Coletta were remembered as *las quemaditas*, the burnt ones. Those who remembered them, their exemplary life, and the supreme sacrifice they made in defense of their virginity and chastity began to pray for their intercession. The local parish church has records documenting prayers answered and favors received through their intercession. They were declared "servants of God" by the Catholic Church, and the process for the canonization of my aunt, Josefa Parra, and her companion, Coletta Melendez, was initiated in Rome in 1965.

The California experience, which had begun for the Lopez family in 1915, proved to be unsatisfying. Mt. Whitney was the highest peak in the continental U.S. and Keeler lies in its shadow. As the sun went down in the west, this mountain seemed to guard our sleepy town. The road to Death Valley, called the mysterious valley, and considered the lowest point in the nation, began at Keeler and could be reached by car in only a few hours. The Alabama Hills, where many Western movies had been filmed, were also in close proximity. The area south and north of Keeler gave evidence to former volcanic activity.

This was indeed an ideal environment for meditation and contemplation, but the barren hills and drying up of Lake Owens in the immediate vicinity contributed to its desolation. This environment was not what Isabel and Severino wanted for their children, the number now having increased to four with the birth of Ramon. As a safeguard for travel and return to Mexico, Severino visited the Mexican consul in Los Angeles to obtain a letter of recommendation, and on November 20, 1920 he and his family crossed the border at Juarez on their way back to La Piedad in Michoacan.

The political situation in Mexico had not yet improved, and the entire nation was still in turmoil. Many of Severino's friends, former friends, and acquaintances were now advocating a movement known as the *Sinarquistas*. This movement made up of fundamentalist Christians provided leadership especially during the government's persecution of the Catholic Church. The *Sinarquistas* nourished the *Cristeros*, who were insurgents from Jalisco, Gaunajuato, and Michoacan. They fought against government troops in defense of their right to worship. The *Cristeros* eventually evolved into the conservative political party that is now referred to in Mexico as P.A.N. (Partido Accion Nacional).

Though not totally involved in the party's activities, Severino was sympathetic to its philosophy, and he promoted the cause through his writings in the city's periodicals. But Severino's main preoccupation at this stage of his life was his growing family. My younger brother Ramon had died, but in 1921 a new baby boy—Peter—was born into our family. Severino made a financial investment in a general merchandise store located on the banks of the Rio Lerma, a river flowing through the city of La Piedad. I still remember that when I walked into the store as a young child my dad would say to me: *Aqui viene el marchante de aprovecho*, meaning, "Here comes a customer who takes advantage." Of course, he was referring to the fact that I quite often asked for some goodies and would then leave without paying for them.

Throughout Mexico there was still much unrest, and power continued to rest in the hands of the revolutionary elite. The constitution had nationalized churches and forbade priests to wear clerical garb in public, to discuss politics, or even vote. Severino became indignant; his editorials were poignant and direct, condemning what he described as Marxist tactics of the government. His friends of earlier years, some of whom were now in high places, warned him that a few leaders were flexing their muscles and that his life was in danger.

Severino, heeding their advice, remained quiet for a while as he prepared to leave the country. He sold his business and made plans for a return to the U.S., being assured his family was safe in the company of Marcelo Parra, his father-in-law. Severino then left for Joliet, Illinois in 1924, where the *paisanos*—fellow Mexicans—had arranged a place for him to stay. During the following year of 1925, my mother and the four of us children joined my father in Joliet.

Into the city: Chicago

1926-1932

South Chicago was the next stop for the Lopez family. A good number of relatives and friends became attracted to the steel mill industry present in the area and job opportunities settling in this diverse ethnic neighborhood. After a few months in Joliet my father decided to move to the South Side of Chicago, and we moved into an apartment within walking distance of Our Lady of Guadalupe Church. A Jesuit priest named Father William Kane, realizing the need to have a place of worship for the increasing number of Mexican Catholics, obtained army barracks and had them transported to 90th and Mackinaw streets in Chicago. He converted the barracks into the first church for Mexican Catholics under the name Our Lady of Guadalupe. Cardinal George Mundelein asked the Claretian Fathers to staff the parish, and in 1925 Father Sebastian Riperor, Father James Tort, and Brother Raymond Pratdesaba were occupying the rear of the church redesigned into living quarters.

Needless to say, the Lopez family soon became involved in

parish activities. My mother became a member of the *Guadalupanas*, and my father joined the St. Vincent de Paul Society. Through that organization he could reach out to the poor. My mother had been preparing me for my First Holy Communion, so I was easily admitted into the group being instructed and made my First Communion in May of 1926.

Upon our arrival in Chicago, my older brother Robert, my sister Charlotte, and I were enrolled at the local public school. There was no bilingual education, but I managed to make myself understood. Four years later I transferred to a Catholic school and, without difficulty, entered the fifth grade. I was able to speak both English and Spanish and finished each year with a fairly good passing grade. Our parents, however, insisted we speak Spanish at home. My father had brought with him a good collection of books, including a large, four-volume *History of Mexico*. As we returned home from school each day we were expected to read or write something in Spanish before going out into the neighborhood.

Don Severino dreamed of going back to Mexico, even though at this period of time he could not give the matter serious thought. Churches were being closed, priests were being executed, and many of his friends had joined the Cristeros uprising, taking up arms in defense of their right to worship. Don Severino decided to publish a simple newsletter, *Avispa* (The Hornet), to inform the large contingency of people in Chicago who were from Jalisco, Guanajuato, and Michoacan what was taking place in Mexico. *Avispa* acted also as a tool of support for the Cristero movement taking place back home. However, his efforts were frustrated when the Mexican hierarchy recommended that the Cristeros lay down their arms and seek a peaceful solution. The *Federales* welcomed the bishop's suggestion and, in turn, proceeded to execute the leaders of the *Cristero* rebellion.

The blazing furnaces lighting the skies at night offered no appeal for my father. He was not interested in being employed by the steel industry, and preferred to rely on his experience as a merchant. So, as always, he placed his faith in divine Providence and established a grocery store, *El Fenix*, giving his customers the option of buying on credit. Most of his clients were well known to him, and throughout the neighborhood there existed a feeling of being all one family. This created a strong element of trust, and he became very successful. Taking on two other partners, they expanded their business to include El Fenix No.2 and El Fenix No.3—located in the neighborhoods of Bush and South Deering, respectively. Everything went fine until the financial crash of October 1929. The steel mills were shut down and, since there was no employment, my dad and his partners were forced to declare bankruptcy. About this time there was a diphtheria epidemic in Chicago that took the lives of two members of our family, Lupe, 3, and Anthony, a child of 1 and a half.

The small building on Mackinaw Avenue was still being used as a church but soon became inadequate as more Mexican families moved into South Chicago. The Claretians, with the approval of the Chicago Archdiocese, built a larger structure on some land donated by Frank J. Lewis, a Knight of St. Gregory. He had also provided a home, adjacent to the church, for the Cordimarian Sisters. Coming from Mexico, these nuns would help in the religious instruction of the immigrant children. The sisters were a great assistance to the Claretian Fathers, as they responded to both the spiritual and social needs of the Mexican immigrants.

When I turned 11 in 1929, my dad allowed me to become a newsboy for *The Chicago Herald Examiner* in the South Shore area, and I developed an awareness of events in other areas of the city. I read first-hand about the effects of Prohibition, the gang feuds between the Morans on the North Side and Al Capone on the South Side, who were all vying for control. I also read about the St. Valentine's Day Massacre on February 14, 1929. Living amid all these dangerous happenings, I did not stray too far from home.

On Saturdays, my brother Peter and I were allowed to see a movie at one of the three local theaters on Commercial Avenue. The Petes Theater featured a movie, usually a Western, for three cents. My brother and I would run back home unaware these movies were probably filmed in the Alabama Hills, not far from my birthplace in the Lone Pine area of California. We made believe we were cowboys by slapping the sides of our corduroy pants to imitate the sound of horses' hooves.

On Black Tuesday in October 1929 was the crash of the stock market, kicking off the Great Depression. South Chicago was greatly affected, as was the rest of the nation. The steel mills were quiet, and though the skies above were blue and beautiful without soot or smoke marring the air, the pockets of the common folks were empty. Nobody was working. Our Lady of Guadalupe Church became a haven for Hispanic immigrants who had made that neighborhood their home. The church basement was transformed into a warehouse where food and clothing, provided by the government and Catholic Charities, were distributed at the beginning of each week. My dad and other St. Vincent de Paul members were in charge of this distribution. The pastor, Father James

Tort reached out to the poor with great faith and trust. He began public devotion to St. Jude with his parishioners, asking this forgotten apostle to intercede in the great needs of his people. Realizing the great response of people toward this devotion, he was encouraged to promote it nationwide. Father Tort established a printing press on the church premises producing letters, pamphlets, and leaflets explaining this devotion. These were circulated through the mail. The initial preparation for these mailings was supervised by the parish secretary and completed by my three friends and me, who were all altar boys. An elaborate shrine was built in the church and approved by Rome. It has been the National Shrine and Center for devotion to St. Jude since 1929. It was and still is visited annually by thousands of faithful people who come to pray. Many now return to give thanks for favors received through the intercession of St. Jude.

The days of the Great Depression did not have much to offer in the way of material things. The U.S. government, in cooperation with Catholic Charities of Chicago, supplied the essential needs of food and clothing. We all became accustomed to wearing hand-me-downs from the older members of the family. Tuition at the Catholic school was only $1 and for more than one sibling the cost was $1.75 per family.

On my wanderings along the 79th Street beach, or Rainbow Beach, which it was called, I discovered a large patch of *verdolagas*, a spinach-like plant used by Mexican families to complement either soup or salad in their daily cuisine. I filled a few dozen small paper bags, and went house-to-house selling my find for a nickel a bag. I proudly handed my profits to my mother to help in the family needs.

My three altar boy friends and I were approximately the

same age and we all attended St. Patrick's Catholic School on Commercial Avenue. We had become close friends, and we were a sorry sight—four little Mexican kids attending a predominantly Irish school. I inherited the name of "Pancho" as I mingled with the Irish lads.

Tragically, Louie, a member of our quartet became a victim of a hit-and-run accident. He was badly hurt and for over a year had to undergo special care. Eventually he was able to walk, but he was left with a slight limp. As soon as he could he rejoined our group as an altar boy at Our Lady of Guadalupe.

At an early age we often talked about what we wanted to be when we grew up. I wanted to become a doctor, but soon lost interest in that vocation after mentioning my desire to the *el campanero*, an elderly man who rang the bells in our steeple. He told me that prior to becoming a doctor, I would have to undergo a test to see if I fulfilled one of the requirements—that of having a cast iron stomach! He said this was necessary because I would have to *chupar la pus*, absorb the infection of a wound orally. The thought of this nauseated me, and I soon dropped the idea of entering the medical field.

About this time Louie revived his idea of becoming a priest, and often spoke about it. Being convinced he was serious, the three of us decided we would all go to the seminary together. Various gangs were being formed in the neighborhood, and I, for one, did not feel a sense of belonging to the "in" crowd. My first feeling of el poche syndrome came when I pondered whether going to the seminary was the right choice.

I don't remember how or when l mentioned this to my parents. My older sister had recently left for San Antonio, Texas to join the Cordimarian Sisters, and I had taken on the chores of caring for my baby sister Carmen, who was only a year and a half. My father, a strong disciplinarian, took my decision in stride. He lectured me at length about discernment. He was an eloquent speaker and throughout my younger life had ruled with an iron hand, according to the old axiom "Spare the rod and spoil the child." On this occasion, however, he was kind and understanding.

    I had always been very close to my mother. From infancy she had taught me my prayers, prepared me for First Holy Communion, and would bless us each day as we took off for school. On Thursday evenings, we would all attend the holy hour at the parish. Ours was a practicing Catholic family rooted in the traditions of Old Mexico. When I approached my mother about my decision, she simply remarked that she would pray, and "God's will would be done." Father Tort, the pastor, had become aware of our intentions and proceeded to make arrangements for admission into the seminary. He decided on the Claretian seminary in Compton, California.

    South Chicago did not have much to offer, but California did. It was 1932: The Olympic games were being held in Los Angeles, and Catalina Island was the spring training camp of our favorite team, the Chicago Cubs. Hollywood was where all the movies came from. This looked great to four 13-year-old kids from Chicago's inner city. So we all agreed to go for it!

    On July 25, the Feast of St. James and also Father Tort's birthday, we all gathered at Our Lady of Guadalupe with our parents. My father took me into the church, and we both knelt in front of Our Lady's image. In a loud and sonorous voice, he spoke to Jesus and the Blessed Mother. He prayed long and eloquently, the sum of his prayer being: "You gave him to me, now I am returning him to you, take good care of him."

A huge crowd accompanied us to the Santa Fe Station, and we boarded the train bound for California. Days later my young brother Benny, accustomed to seeing me leave home each morning to serve Mass, simply asked my parents, "When is Sevy coming home? When is the Mass going to be over?"

I had been on the train only an hour when I began to get homesick. The Lopez family had always been close, and I missed them! My closest friends were with me, but I still felt lonely. Those three and a half days in a chair car were made bearable by the beautiful panorama seen through the broad windows of the train. As a teenager, I had never stepped outside Chicago. I was now admiring the great cornfields of Illinois, the wheat that swayed with the wind in Kansas, and the plains of Texas. The train made a stop in Albuquerque, New Mexico, and I marveled at the Indians selling their trinkets. All we had to barter with were fruit and tacos wrapped in heavy cellophane. I had never been beyond Chicago but was now given an opportunity to see much of the countryside.

We arrived at Los Angeles the morning of Friday, July 29. Two major seminarians were there at the station to receive us and drive us to our new home, Dominguez Memorial Seminary, approximately 15 miles from Los Angeles. During the colonization of California, the King of Spain had made a land grant to the Dominguez family. This grant stretched from the Pacific Ocean to what is now the City of Los Angeles. Through secularization and admission of California to the Union, this family had lost most of its land. They had built a large ranch, which was eventually made available to the Claretians with a stipulation that it be used for the education of priests.

California seminary
1932-1944

As we drove inside the grounds I became breathless. I had grown accustomed to the "asphalt jungle" of South Chicago and its scarcity of trees. Here, however, the entrance road was lined with large Magnolia trees and spacious lawns. The fragrance of sweet orange blossoms filled the air, and at a distance beyond the entrance were large Sycamore and Poplar trees.

We were eventually introduced to the prefect of postulants, and our life as high school seminarians began. That night as I lay in bed, after having said night prayers in the chapel with all 32 of the minor seminarians, I could think only of Adam and Eve. They must have been here before the fall. I kept on saying to myself: *Aqui me quedo!*—"I'm staying here!" The teeming street life of Chicago would be only a memory. I was about to begin a remote preparation for the priesthood, in peace and quiet.

The seminary grounds were divided into two sections, one for the professed who had already taken their vows and another for those in the philosophy department. They occupied the old homestead that had been the home of the Dominguez Family during the romantic era of California. The other, larger section of the two-story building had been erected later. It housed the high school students and the faculty. The grounds included a baseball diamond, a handball court, and an outdoor swimming pool, and during the remaining summer days we made good use of these facilities.

In late August, shortly before the beginning of the school year, the assistant prefect asked if I'd like anything sent back to Chicago. He informed me that two of our group of four were going back. I didn't understand because both of them were happy, and, in fact, one of the two had tears in his eyes as we said goodbye. The reason for their leaving was never told to me, but as time went by, I drew my own conclusion, which I will later explain.

The curriculum of the minor seminary was that of a high school and the daily timetable, though heavy, was conducive to studying and learning. There were four classes a day and a study period before each class. Latin was given special emphasis, and at the end of the four-year course we were expected to master this language by speaking fluently and being able to express ourselves. Consequently, *Caesar's Gallic Wars* and *Cicero* were hashed and rehashed, as well as *Krause's Modern Latin Conversation*. All of our studies that year were geared as a preparation for courses in philosophy and theology. A lot of studying and learning took place, but in retrospect I doubt whether the entire system complied with the California state requirements for high school.

Silence was a requirement throughout the day, except during the half-hour recreation periods that followed each meal, and a one-hour period in the afternoon. There were no classes on Sundays, holidays, or Wednesday afternoons, but we were not allowed to leave the premises. The discipline taught to me by my parents became valuable as I coped with the strict timetable of minor seminary life.

A small book of rules called *The Mirror* clearly spelled out the expectations of us. Touching in any form was forbidden, consequently contact sports were not allowed, nor were friendships termed "particular friendships." I presumed this was an effort to avoid familiarity, but it was almost ridiculous to see high school students playing touch football with foot-long taggers. We sublimated, though, and became accustomed to this unusual way of life.

On March 10, 1933 Southern California experienced a strong earthquake, a 7.5 on the Richter scale. At 5 p.m. the entire building shook while I was attending class, and a piano in the classroom came rolling across the floor. I had never experienced an earthquake, and my first thought was that the boiler had burst. I tried to exit through a place where a window used to be. Eventually we all exited and gathered in the large space between buildings that were still intact, but showing tremendous cracks. That evening we slept out on the ball field. The major seminarians had previously gone into the building to salvage pillows and blankets. We felt aftershocks all throughout the night, and the sound of ambulances kept us awake. While thousands were killed from the earthquake, there were no fatalities among the seminarians, although one was injured by falling bricks as he rushed out of the Dominguez Homestead. Both seminary buildings were condemned, and arrangements were made for us to spend the following few days at San Gabriel Mission, where we occupied a large auditorium.

Eventually, the postulants and major seminarians left for Phoenix, where we occupied a vacated parochial school while repairs were being made on both seminary buildings. It was June 1933, the intense desert heat of Phoenix had begun, and Immaculate Heart of Mary School was not air-conditioned. The stifling heat was becoming unbearable and some of the seminarians became ill. As soon as repairs on the seminary buildings were approved by the State of California, we returned and normal seminary life was restored.

In October of the same year another earthquake shook the area. Though not as strong as the previous one, this one devastated our building. The building was condemned, and the minor seminary program was again transferred to Phoenix. On this occasion, a good number of our seminarians would not accept the challenge of a second call to Spartan living and left for home. Though inconvenient, this hiatus was at least bearable. The directors allowed us to participate in some of the parish activities, especially during the Lenten season and Holy Week services. A weekly excursion to the desert became part of our weekly activities, giving us an opportunity for some physical exercise as we climbed Mt. Camelback.

During our stay in Arizona, the Claretian order realized that a more adequate place for the minor seminary program was required. They purchased property in Walnut, California from a Hollywood actress named Mary Pickford. It was nestled in a picturesque spot at the foot of the Puente Hills and was used by the actress to entertain. The complex included cottages and an administration building on eight acres of land overlooking a vast valley of grapefruit, orange, and walnut trees. At a distance and visibly clear, was a young range of mountains and Mt. San Antonio, popularly known as Mt. Baldy.

As soon as the school year came to a close we made our way to Silver Peak—the name of our new home. The only drawback to our new location was that it had no grounds for athletics. Most of us being "jocks" and sports-minded, we soon leveled a hill and made a provisional softball diamond with additional room for a dirt basketball court. The surrounding hills were ideal for our weekly hike and a chance to clear our minds.

This was my second year in the minor seminary program, and upon entering into my third year, I began to analyze my situation. I had noticed the attitude of some of our directors, which made things a bit unpleasant. Most of them were Spaniards who had been brought to this country to direct the training of seminarians. At that time, the directors of seminaries in Spain, France, and Ireland were tinged with a bit of Jansenistic piety and were inflexibly rigorous. Jansenism was characterized by the belief that human nature was corrupt and affected a divorce between the spirit and the flesh. These directors believed humanity had to be kept in check by penitential rigor. *The Mirror of the Postulants*, the book of regulations aforementioned, gave evidence to this Jansenistic piety. Many of us considered several of the laws a bit strange but at the time were not smart enough to detect this Jansenistic approach to our training, We did, however, rebel in our behavior.

Another attitude eventually became noticeable—it was *de facto* racism toward a good number of Mexican students. This became so evident that a number of seminarians left the seminary, even though they had been certain of their call to the priesthood.

Later on, after my ordination, I was told by an elderly Claretian and a provincial superior about an unpleasant situation taking place in the beginning years of our province. They said we were becoming polarized. The pioneers had come to the U.S. at the request of the bishops to assist them in the Hispanic apostolate. As they became pastors in Mexican parishes, they sent candidates to the seminary. A good number of Spanish priests, specifically those in charge of formation, were of the opinion that greater efforts should be made to establish a purely American province, toward Anglo-Saxon candidates, *los hueros*, "the light ones." This, I thought, explained the early departure of my two friends from Chicago. Given this general attitude, it was fortunate for my friend and myself that our skin happened to be of a lighter hue. I had inherited light skin from my mother, *la Huera*, and my friend was from Guanajuato where a good number of French had settled during the time of Maximilian. Having experienced such discrimination brought with it another incident of el poche syndrome—the feeling that I do and do not belong.

An interesting incident occurred during my time in Silver Peak. On one of our hikes throughout the hills, the prefect went with two or three seminarians to fill some sacks with compost for his plants. The others and myself headed for the hills, but a third group went by a farmhouse and was attracted to some horses. They jumped the fences and began to ride the ponies. The owner caught them and sought out the prefect to make his complaint. The prefect verbally castigated the offenders and remarked that they, as penance, had to carry the sacks of compost back to the seminary. I smiled, thinking that, for a change, I had not been with the group of troublemakers. The prefect then looked over to where I was and said, "You too, Lopez." When I protested, the prefect replied, "Lopez, if you had been with them, you too would have gotten on the steeds!" I quietly went along with the prefect's injunction, recognizing that he was probably right but complied for the most part because I had, perhaps on previous occasions, transgressed and not been caught.

Among the many rules in seminary, the rule of silence was one of my great obstacles, as was that of avoiding personal contact in sports. On one occasion I found a pair of boxing gloves in an abandoned cottage and challenged one of the seminarians. We sparred for a couple of rounds. Afterward, realizing a seminarian would have seen us on a monitor and no doubt report us, we went to the prefect and pleaded guilty. Our penance for the next three evenings was to kneel prior to supper in the dining room and publicly state that we had broken the rule of *The Mirror:* "Thou shalt not touch, not even in sports." A similar penance was imposed upon a group who decided to play tackle football, and, as usual, I was among them.

The third member of our original foursome from Chicago became disenchanted with seminary life and decided to leave after two years. I had become accustomed to this new style of life and loved the surroundings, keeping in mind that inconveniences and strictness were part and parcel of our education.

During the summer months, the seminarians, most of whom came from California, were allowed to spend one week at home with their family. Being from Chicago I had to remain alone, but was given permission to raid the fruit trees. I developed a tremendous taste for the juicy persimmons and to this day seek out the farmers' markets for this delicious fruit.

I developed an interest in sports as well, which the Spanish priests could not understand. My love for sports, as my prefect pointed out, was "an inordinate attachment to the world." He would, however, allow us to listen to the radio on Sundays and made a copy of the sports page available once it had been censored. (They cut out all the pictures of women in print.) Some of us made contraband crystal sets and tuned in to sports programs to keep abreast with the progress of the Chicago Cubs and Notre Dame.

In 1933 the Claretians opened a minor seminary in Momence, Illinois, approximately 40 miles from Chicago, at a farmhouse donated to the order. It drew a few young men. In 1934 some of these men were sent to join the existing program at Silver Peak. Their arrival was a shot in the arm for me, since I was now able to talk about the old hometown and get a personal description of the "Century of Progress" World Fair being held in Chicago that year.

On the fourth year of minor seminary life, those of us who were seniors were given a remote preparation for the novitiate. We had to write a formal request to the provincial and his council for admission and approval to the novitiate. Every Sunday we would join the prefect prior to the noon meal to recite the same noonday prayers recited by the professed members of the order. The prefect would give us a brief talk on what it meant to be a religious, but sadly enough not too much had been told to us about the priesthood during those formative years. The directors made especially sure we did not speak to girls, or as they put it, "to persons of the opposite sex." As a result of this restriction, we felt isolated from people. We had learned a great deal of Latin, Greek, English Composition, and Prosody. We prayed a lot, but the priesthood still remained a dream of something remote and far away.

The seniors were looking forward to the novitiate, and, as beautiful as California was, we were anxious to move from Silver Peak to San Marcos, Texas. I finished my four years of postulancy there. The only communication I had had with my family was through an occasional letter that my dad and mother would send. My father's letters were masterpieces and continually encouraged me to keep going. There were no indications from my directors that I would have the opportunity to visit my family prior to the start of my novitiate, and so I simply conformed to this rule of silence. During these four years of formation, our directors insisted on "detachment from our families." We were teenagers, just out of high school, and felt their efforts were to dehumanize us. I went along with the system, since I was a good distance from my family, but deep down I felt something was wrong. el poche syndrome was beginning to affect me more often.

That year the superiors decided the novitiate program should be transferred back to California. The building at the Dominguez seminary site, originally occupied by the minor seminary, was condemned by the state after the second earthquake. It was repaired and subsequently determined earthquake-proof. The college department and theology students were now occupying it, leaving the homestead building available for the Novitiate Program. In the year 1932, when my three friends and I came from Chicago to the minor seminary, there were 21 who entered. Four years later only three of us "survived" and were approved for the one-year novitiate.

On July 15 we began our year in the novitiate. For these 12 months we would not have formal studies, it was a time given to us by the church to study the *Rules of the Claretian Order*. The three vows of chastity, poverty, and obedience would be explained to us, and we would be given an opportunity to learn about the religious life. The novice master, a kind and elderly man, drilled us as best he could on these subjects and provided spiritual counseling. He was also minister of the entire seminary complex and as such he had the added responsibility of caring for the farm. Consequently, my classmates and I were given the chores of feeding the chickens, rabbits, and livestock. We would also help to bail the hay and assist in the overall care of the farm. The little office of the Blessed Virgin was recited three times a day.

On November 11 the novice master asked me to go with a mechanic who had come to repair our tractor that was an old Fordson model. The mechanic had recently undergone an operation, so he asked if I would crank up the tractor. I agreed and gave it a whirl, but it did not start. Then I pressed down on the crank, and it threw me about five yards. As I recovered from the initial shock, I noticed that my right wrist had been broken. I spent the next three months with my arm in a cast. After six months, a different novice master was appointed. He was also a member of the Claretian provincial council. The continuity of our program suffered because of his occasional absence, as he was often called to Rome for meetings of the General Chapter of the Claretian Order.

With extra praying, meditating, and pious reading during this year it was presumed our spirituality was healthier. We were approved to make our vows of poverty, chastity, and obedience. I doubted very much whether we had captured the full significance of these vows, but since they were temporary we would be given the opportunity at a later time to grow in understanding of their implications.

On July 16, 1937, the anniversary of the founding of the

Claretian order (also the Feast of Our Lady of Mt. Carmel) and at the young age of 18, I made my first religious profession of vows to the Congregation of the Sons of the Immaculate Heart of Mary founded by St. Anthony Mary Claret. I could now attach the letters C.M.F. (which stands for *Cordis Mariae Filius*, or Son of the Heart of Mary) to my name and move across to the building to where my journey began five years prior to this date. Now, however, I would be in the company of professed students studying philosophy and theology.

On July 18, 1936, civil war was declared in Spain, and for the ensuing years there existed a period of great unrest. This conflict had been brewing since 1931 when Spain changed from a monarchy to a republic. The new government introduced laws, agrarian reforms, and attitude changes that exerted much influence on the Catholic Church. Strikes and minor uprisings were the order of the day. The government, also called the Popular Front Movement, was described as a godless movement that acted recklessly.

I have never really understood the politics behind a conflagration responsible for the martyrdom of 58 Claretian priests and seminarians in Barbastro, Catalonia. In the U.S. it polarized the Claretians, most of whom were Spaniards from different provinces of Spain. Some were supporters of the Nationalist insurgents, led by General Francisco Franco, and did not defend the godless regime of the Loyalists, but neither did they agree with the atrocities of Franco who stamped out the separatist movement. Though these supporters belonged to the same religious order and province, some displayed a certain degree of animosity. Consequently the provincial superior and his council decided upon certain necessary transfers of personnel. These were made, and a different climate became evident, especially in the formation program. This was also the year in which the first North American seminarians were ordained to the priesthood. They were influential in the gradual disappearance of Jansenistic piety from the climate of seminary life.

The remaining months of the post-noviciate summer were pleasant ones for my classmates and me. Since the class schedule did not begin until September, we enjoyed the relative leisure and soon became acquainted with the entire group of professed seminarians. The philosophy students were still in temporary vows. The others were perpetually professed, studying theology and subjects directly connected with the priesthood, and their ministry. As a pastime each seminarian was given a portion of the spacious lawns and gardens to maintain. Swimming in our outdoor pool, tennis, and handball were all available to us during these remaining months.

We began classes with the opening of the school year after being away from serious studies for the entire year of our noviciate. In mid-September a solemn Mass of the Holy Spirit was celebrated, and all the professors made "Oaths against Modernism," an oath introduced by Pope Pius IX which all the professors of seminary life were required to take. For the next three years philosophy was to be our major with an emphasis on the science of logic for the first year. It all sounded very interesting but, as we were forewarned, the philosophy class was given in Latin and the textbook was written by a German. After four years of Latin in the minor seminary, I thought I had mastered the language quite well. But when confronted with abstract concepts it became quite a challenge. We did manage to conceptualize the science of logic and passed, using the right words for answers in the tests and reports in class. The second year was not as easy, since we were to discuss metaphysics, the "system of first principles," or humanity's place in nature. These concepts were difficult to understand as explained by our German author, especially because they were written in Latin; but again we managed.

The third year of philosophy, dedicated to the study of ethics, was intellectually challenging, and we all needed an escape. We had a good sports program that provided an opportunity to rest our minds. We organized intramural fast-pitch softball games, as well as touch football and basketball.

In the spring we scheduled an intramural softball game that would determine who would be on the team the following week when we played against the inmates at Terminal Island Federal Prison. I had been designated team captain, and I noticed that as the game progressed the shortstop was finding it difficult to adjust to his position. I asked him if he would rather play my position in left field, to which he agreed, so I took his place at shortstop. Soon after I felt a strong pain on my chin as if something had hit me. I assumed a pebble must have flown off a batter's shoe as he went running by. A few days later, though, I noticed the wound began to fester and would not heal. At the prefect's recommendation I went to a doctor who pried open the wound and discovered a bullet! I had been shot with a .22 bullet that had lodged in my chin, probably from a hunter's rifle in the nearby Dominguez Hills.

As sports helped to clear our minds, the scheduled prayers throughout the day, as well as receiving the Eucharist, sustained our spirit. The last Friday of every month was a day of retreat, always held in silence. During the third year of my religious profession I was strolling silently in the gardens, feeling in a funk throughout the day. Then, as if I had been struck by lightning, a state of paralyzing fear and timidity came over me, and I again began to consider my situation. What am I doing with my life? Am I simply flowing along with time? Do I actually belong here? If I continue in this type of life, not being called, will I mess up my life? On the other hand if I really belong here and then leave, will I be making a mistake? I found myself in a spiritual vacuum, and it was sucking up my life. I began to cry. I felt I needed a breath of the Spirit to restore my motivation!

It came like a quiet breeze: Seven years earlier I left Chicago with three companions, and all of them had since returned. I realized that if God had not called me, I, too, would have been gone. That dark night of the soul had all but disappeared as the brightness of the moment allowed me to see things in a different perspective. I was now convinced that I belonged and was determined to continue. Through God's inspiration I had been able to overcome my latest bout with an el poche moment.

Thus in 1940, prior to entering the theology department and at the age of 21, I made my perpetual vows, promising to be a Claretian the rest of my life.

Theology classes, though conducted in Latin, were somewhat more interesting than the philosophy courses we had just finished. As we proceeded with dogma and moral theology, I began to see the larger picture and looked anxiously toward the remaining years of my training and ordination. About this time a group of students just concluding their novitiate from the Claretian province of Mexico arrived at our seminary. They were entering our philosophy and theology program and they spoke no English, so I was assigned to instruct them. I considered this a marvelous opportunity to regain my confidence in speaking Spanish. We had been forbidden to speak Spanish during minor seminary days, and as a consequence I found myself speaking a bit awkwardly.

A letter arrived from my parents informing me that my uncle, my mother's brother who lived in San Fernando, would soon be coming to the seminary for a visit. He was the same uncle who had been present at my birth in Keeler, and he had remained in Southern California to work for the railroad. He and his family of four daughters and two sons came to visit occasionally. I would have enjoyed my uncle's family during my four years of minor seminary life, but, alas, it was only after my perpetual vows that they appeared on the scene. God's ways are not always our ways.

Around that time, my younger brother Peter decided to become a Claretian lay brother and arrived at the seminary to begin his aspirancy, the time required before entering the novitiate. I was happy to see my brother after seven years, and of course delighted over his choice to become a Claretian. There was a strictness associated with the separation of sections: The priests did not mingle with the seminarians, nor were the seminarians allowed to mingle with the novices or lay brothers. Occasionally, after he had made his first vows and served the community as cook and dietician, I was able to meet with my brother. During these years the Claretian lay brothers were not provided opportunities for growth and development. As a result my brother became disenchanted with the daily routine. He left the Claretians and is now a happily married man with a family.

With the bombing of Pearl Harbor on December 7, 1941, our country entered into war. Our seminary, because it was so close to the Pacific Ocean, was greatly affected. We all went to the military recruitment center in Compton and were classified as 4D, the classification given to divinity students who were exempt from the draft.

We did, however, join in the war effort as one of our seminarians, appointed as precinct captain, would attend information meetings designed to inform citizens as to what they could do. We were told to avoid turning on lights in the seminary grounds at certain hours and similar things. On one occasion we saw an unfamiliar object in the sky and then we heard all the anti-aircraft guns on the coast. Many of our lawns were converted into victory gardens, and we grew vegetables. I recall that during this effort we had an abundant harvest of sweet potatoes.

Actually, one of our seminarians decided to do a little more toward the war effort. One morning he neatly folded his cassock, which we all wore, placed it at the entrance of the seminary, and left to join the Army. We never heard from him again, and to this day I do not know how he fared. Two of our priests became Army chaplains, and one of them went through the entire African campaign, Sicily, and Anzio.

During these final years of theology we had an opportunity to engage in some ministry. A classmate and I would go every Sunday morning to a children's hospital in Norwalk, about 15 miles away, where all the children were victims of polio. We would wheel them to a nearby church for Mass, teach them catechism, and entertain them for some time. The pastor of the local church, wanting to show us his appreciation, offered to take us to a nearby theater to see the current movie, *Casablanca*. The superior granted us permission with the condition we'd be back for supper. As a consequence we had to leave the theater early without knowing what happened to Humphrey Bogart at the end of the movie.

During one summer we were sent to Jerome, Arizona, a small mining town north of Prescott. In those years this town was a thriving little establishment, teeming with people working in the copper mines to supply a mineral that was in great demand during the war years. The town was built on the side of a mountain overlooking the lush Verde Valley. When a storm would form, we could see lightning striking below in the areas out toward Oak Creek Canyon. We ran a summer school program for about 200 children in an abandoned school building. On Tuesday evenings the people in the town played well-organized, fast-pitch softball games, providing a marvelous opportunity for these hard working people to come together in friendly competition and relax in a community atmosphere. My classmate and I were eager to join them, but the pastor, a priest who had been in our formation program during earlier years, would not allow us out of the rectory during the evening hours.

At various times after our perpetual vows we received the tonsure, a ceremony characterized by the clipping of our hair on top of our heads, leaving only the hair around the sides. This ceremony symbolized our admission into the clerical state and was, over a course of time, followed by the reception of minor orders: acolyte and lector.

Beginning with our fourth year of theology we were instructed to prepare for major orders, the reception of the sub-diaconate, and in December 1943 we joined a class of Franciscan seminarians in Santa Barbara for this purpose. Sub-diaconate gave us the privilege to assist the celebrant at a Solemn High Mass, and also imposed on us an obligation to recite the *Divine Office* or *Prayer of Breviary*. The *Breviary* was written in Latin and was divided into various sections to be recited throughout the day: Matins and lauds in the morning, the minor hours—-prime, terce, sext and none—before noon, and Vespers and Compline in the evening. This responsibility, which was morally obliging, added to our class preparation and made for a hectic schedule. We received the order of the diaconate, the second of the major orders, in March of 1944. Normally, more time would have been given for the conferring of these orders, but we were in an accelerated program due to the war and it resulted in unusual pressure.

May 28, 1944 was set as the date for our ordination to the priesthood, and we began a 10-day retreat to prepare for this sacrament. I had informed my family in Chicago and received word that my mother, and younger brother Ben would be coming for the ceremony. I had received details concerning their arrival. Since I had not seen any member of my family for more than 12 years, I approached the provincial superior in joyful anticipation to ask permission to go to the train station and meet them. He looked up from his desk, and with a stern look and angry voice he replied, "Go back to your retreat and stop thinking of your family. Give thought to your ordination!" He must have reconsidered because the retreat master eventually informed me that I could go to Union Station and receive my mother and brother. Perhaps he remembered I had been separated from them for an extraordinary length of time.

Ordination

1944

St. Vibiana Cathedral in Los Angeles was filled to capacity with friends and relatives of those about to be ordained. Los Angeles Archbishop John Cantwell was the ordaining bishop. There were 21 candidates for the priesthood, mostly diocesan, but the group included two of us who were Claretians. The Mass and the entire ceremony lasted close to three hours. I was so intent upon doing the right thing during the complicated liturgy that I did not ponder enough upon the sublime meaning of each individual action. One of the first acts performed after the ceremony by a newly ordained priest is to impart his blessing on the bishop, the priests present in the sanctuary, and the members of his immediate family. My mother had waited 12 years for this moment, and as she knelt quietly at the communion rail I blessed her. And after the bishop consecrated my forefingers with oil, I gave my mother the gauze that had bound my fingers on each hand. Then she kissed the palm of my hands. These were touching moments for me and made more meaningful as I remembered my mother washing my hands as a child prior to sitting at the table for the family meal.

As we drove from the cathedral, heading back to the seminary, I felt more relaxed and became aware of the extensive urban renewal that transformed the area around St. Vibiana. Old Chinatown had been torn down to make room for a new Union Station and more trains to arrive and depart. An alternate Chinatown was now rising in the distance.

I thought, "How symbolic! I was ordained on the eve of Pentecost, when the Holy Spirit transformed the apostles into new men, and by the same Holy Spirit I had been transformed into a priest of God."

The following day I celebrated my first Mass at the seminary chapel with my mother, my brother, and relatives from San Fernando all present. On the following Sunday, the pastor of the Old Plaza Church in Los Angeles, who had been prefect during my earlier training, invited me to celebrate my first High Mass at that historic church. Soon after I made arrangements to return to Chicago where I would celebrate my first official Mass at Our Lady of Guadalupe Church. I was requested to stop at Phoenix, where I had spent some time as a seminarian following the earthquake in California, to celebrate Mass at the Immaculate Heart of Mary Parish for a large Hispanic congregation. A newly ordained priest of Mexican descent was a rarity in those days, and the pastor of this church was now anxious to present me to his flock as an ordained priest.

I was a bit apprehensive about my homecoming to the South Chicago Parish I had left 12 years earlier. True, many of the young men I had grown up with were presently in the Armed Forces, but I had no doubt many of the old timers would still remember me and some of the mischief of my early childhood years. My fears were assuaged, however, when on June 15 I celebrated Mass at 9 a.m. for the St. Jude Police League on their Communion Sunday and at noon at Our Lady of Guadalupe. The church was filled to capacity. Mass during those years was still said in Latin, and the celebrant stood with his back to the people.

As I looked up at the picture of Our Lady of Guadalupe enshrined above the altar on the wall, I could but simply thank Our Lady for having answered the prayers of my father, who 12 years earlier on this very same spot had asked her to guide and guard me as I left for the seminary in California.

Beginning of ministry
1944-1946

I was allowed one week with my family after my first Mass celebration and then told to report to St. Francis Church in Chicago. This church had been built by German immigrants and survived the Great Chicago Fire, but now the parish was 100 percent Mexican, which provided a great field for my ministry. The Claretians had been ministering there since 1927, and the services performed by the Spanish priests who continued to staff the parish had converted the neighborhood into a vibrant community.

This was my first assignment, and very soon I became involved. I was asked to assume the position of youth director, and I accepted. A group of high school students would meet periodically to edit a parish newspaper, which they titled *The Crier*. They would send copies to the boys in the Armed Forces to keep them informed of activities and the news from our parish. I extended a helping hand, which allowed the youth group to broaden their activities.

During these war years we did our best to keep our young

people occupied through social activities and sports. A group of teenagers, who went by the name of "Wildcats," were instrumental in keeping these activities alive. This organization still exists in the city as a fraternity and continues to perform charitable work.

On one occasion, through a bit of persuasion, I was able to obtain free admission to the Ringling Brothers Circus for the entire parochial school. But since we had insufficient funds for the rental of buses, we decided to walk to the stadium—a good eight blocks away. Monitors and crossing guards were well drilled for the occasion, and for the entire way to the circus the school children behaved wonderfully.

Getting back was another story as they had seen the circus and were completely satisfied. To get them to return to school in an orderly fashion turned out to be a gargantuan task with every child going every which way! All I could do was to pray that nothing would happen to them, and we finally made it to the school without a mishap.

These were war years, so our youth was continually saying farewell to friends leaving for active service. A holy hour was held on Thursday evenings to pray for all our men and women in uniform. One of the side altars in the church was completely filled with pictures of these soldiers brought in by mothers and sweethearts. Each week this service was well attended at the church as the community prayed for the safe return of family members and good friends, as well as those unknown. The parish was active, and this served as occupational therapy for my first year as a priest. It was especially instrumental in helping me cope with the sudden changes of moving from Southern California to Chicago, but also of my new role as a priest.

Prior to returning to Chicago, I had spent many years in a clean, healthy atmosphere, surrounded by gardens and breathing country air. I was now an inner-city resident, just one block away from Maxwell Street, famous at that time for its raucous activities and rancid atmosphere. Most of the homes in that area were heated by coal, and soot filled the air. The alleys were overloaded with garbage, and huge rats would challenge any pedestrian or vehicle disturbing their habitat. I lost my appetite and with it a considerable amount of weight. On one occasion I was summoned to an apartment building that I might attend to a person who evidently had died that evening. I walked into an ice-cold apartment and saw the man lying in bed. I moved his arm, and his whole body moved! He was completely frozen.

Eventually things improved. A large two-story building adjacent to the church was purchased by the parish and converted into a rectory with adequate offices and living quarters. Upon my appointment to St. Francis, the provincial superior had told the pastor I should not be allowed to see my family too often, except on birthdays and other special occasions. My father, however, would occasionally take public transportation from the South Side and visit. The provincial was a good and saintly man who still believed in enforcing the old monastic ways of some of our communities in Spain. I was glad that my pastor did not take him seriously.

Normally changes in personnel appointments were made in our province every three years. I had been at St. Francis for only one year when the new assignments were published. I was to report to a Claretian parish in El Paso, Texas. But I had a premonition that somehow I would not get to El Paso, and just as I had suspected I was soon informed by the prefect of studies in the province that I should proceed instead to the Catholic University of America in Washington, D.C. I was to take a six-week course in what he referred to as "sacred eloquence," since the wartime-accelerated program at the seminary had not provided me an opportunity to do so. The course turned out to be very instructive and helpful. The professors were very qualified, one of them having been an actor on Broadway and another a renowned Dominican homilist. To this day I remember their useful instructions on delivering the Word of God.

During the six weekends in Washington, I was asked to accompany my former pastor, Father Joaquin De Prada, who had moved to Trenton, New Jersey in response to a request from the bishop to help minister to Mexicans working on the railroads. Through an arrangement made with the respective governments, these men had come from Mexico to the U.S. to supply the workforce needed during the war. They were called *braceros*. After the six-week course I was asked to move to the Trenton cathedral rectory with another Claretian priest, an elderly man. Eventually the diocese acquired a home for us. Our responsibility was to now answer the spiritual needs of men stationed at the various camps throughout New Jersey along the Reading Railroad Line. On Sunday morning I would celebrate 6 a.m. Mass at the Trenton camp, then drive up to New Brunswick for 9 a.m. Mass, and then on to Metuchen for a noon Mass.

This schedule was a bit demanding, especially since the law of fasting from midnight the night prior to saying Mass or receiving the Eucharist, was to be observed. We also were not allowed to have any nourishment between Masses. A few years later this law was relaxed, and priests were allowed to take something *per modum potus*, in liquid form, between Masses. During the week I would visit the men in these camps, provide some religious and social activities, and try to help out wherever I could. This program came to an end in February 1946, though, because the war had ended and so the men returned to Mexico. Bishop William A. Griffin of Trenton invited us to remain in his diocese if we could find ministry among the Spanish-speaking, However, my elderly companion was not too interested, especially having just experienced an intensely cold winter. Soon after that I received orders to report to San Gabriel Mission in California.

Left: *The Lopez family, 1922. Severino is 2nd from left, age 3.*

Right: *The four future seminarians, July 1932. Clockwise from left: Roy Bautista, Sevy Lopez, Louie Chavez, James Mendoza.*

Left: *Sevy, age 8, on his First Communion day.*

Above: *Josefa Parra, Sevy's aunt whose cause is being considered for sainthood.*

In front of Our Lady of Guadalupe Parish, 1930. Sevy is the altar boy at top right.

The Dominguez Seminary baseball team. Sevy is in the back row, 2nd from right.

Left: *Goofing around on the basketball court, Dominguez Seminary. Sevy is at center.*

63

Father Severino Lopez, C.M.F. with his mother and father on his ordination day, 1944.

"By the Grace of God, a Priest forever."

A Remembrance

of my

Priestly Ordination

and

First Holy Mass

May 28-29, 1944

Rev. Severin Lopez, C. M. F.

"O Jesus, bless my parents, relatives, friends, and all those who have helped me to Thy Holy Altar."

First Mass, Our Lady of Guadalupe 1944.

64

Top: *Giving Communion at one of his first Masses.*

Bottom: *Celebrating a wedding.*

The Lopez family, 1944

Isabel Parra Lopez

Don Severino Lopez

Celebrating his Mexican heritage and having fun.

With fellow Claretian Patrick McPolin.

At the Claretian mission in Tierra Nueva, Mexico, 2002.

In the jubilee year of his priesthood, 1994.

California and Texas

1946-1953

San Gabriel Mission is one of the 21 missions founded in California by Junipero Serra, a Franciscan missionary. It was established in 1771 and has been under the administration of the Claretians since 1908. I was happy to hear of my new assignment since this parish had become a center of Catholic life in the San Gabriel Valley. Many families who had migrated from the East and Midwest after the war had made the San Gabriel Valley their home. They and the old California families made the mission an active and alive parish. Thousands of visitors arrived each year from areas around the country to visit the mission and admire the great work accomplished by the early Franciscans. California in the early '40s still retained much of its pristine romance of the "Days of the Padres," and the mission was greatly instrumental in keeping this spirit alive. Its annual fiesta, held in September to commemorate its founding, was a joyous occasion. There was a local parade preceded by a ball and the crowning of the fiesta queen.

The parish had built an outdoor bowl within the mission grounds, which was the locale for the yearly presentation of "The Bells of San Gabriel," a production written by Cora Montgomery. In music, dance, and dialogue it brought back to life the thrilling heritage of early Californians and a forgotten chapter in the history of the mission. I can still remember the fiery performance of Madeleine Lifur, a consummate Flamenco dancer and member of the mission parish. She and her partner, Raoul Ramirez, were well known throughout California for their professional rendition of folkloric dances of Andalusia.

The parochial school with its 400 children kept me well occupied. I organized an athletic program for both boys and girls. We entered the diocesan Catholic Youth Organization, and the children responded wonderfully. Their prowess was rewarded as they won many trophies for their school. I also reached out to other areas in the parish and enjoyed going into the ethnic neighborhoods where many of our parishioners lived. On the Feast of Our Lady of Guadalupe I would hop on a Model A Ford pickup truck early in the morning and head out to awaken our Hispanic parishioners for the singing of *Las Mañanitas* to Our Lady at the old mission church. The parish was a happy mix of both English-speaking and Hispanic parishioners.

The next tri-annual shifting of personnel found me assigned to Our Lady of Soledad, a completely Hispanic parish in the heart of East Los Angeles, known as *Maravilla* among the younger Mexican folk. The *Pachuco* phenomenon, so prominent during the war years among Mexican youth was tapering off, but I was still exposed to some of its oddities as I became more involved with the neighborhood youth. For example, they had been so neglected and ostracized by society during the war years that they had responded by drawing attention through outlandish dress and a particular way of speaking. This attitude did more to isolate them and make them a target of society. Deep down they were good kids, and our job was to show them that God loved them. Eventually they grew out of this strange sociological oddity.

Youth work continued to be my main preoccupation. A boxing program started by Father Louie Vasquez, who preceded me, drew a good number of aficionados. A semi-professional football team was also formed to attract young men returning home from the Army. I was proud of this team which performed so well and showed proficiency in sports. But on one occasion they met their match.

We organized a parish picnic at the Dominguez seminary grounds, where I had studied. The "Soledad Crusaders," as the football team was named, decided on a touch football game with the seminarians. What a mistake! The well-disciplined seminarians not only ran circles around our men but their no-nonsense blocking forced a good number of our men out of the game. All I could say was: "How things have changed." In my days of seminary life, we were not even allowed to touch each other!

On Easter Monday in 1949, I received a phone call from our provincial informing me that I should transfer to San Antonio, Texas. At a group outing a young Claretian priest, Father Albert Daube, had drowned trying to save a member of the Newman Club high-school youth group from San Fernando Cathedral. I was to take up the work that he had begun at the cathedral parish.

The Claretians came to San Antonio in 1902 at the request of that diocese's bishop. He had appointed the Claretians as his assistants and they directed the parish from the bishop's residence. Two years later they moved into the Immaculate Heart of Mary Rectory and supervised the cathedral's activities from that newly constructed Claretian community. In October 1914 they were able to move into the cathedral's old rectory. It seemed as if the ministry at the San Fernando Cathedral had been fashioned just for me. A modern gymnasium had recently been built to be used by the parish, the parochial school, and the girls' high school. A program for its use had to be designed, and organizing this project put me in touch with some wonderful members of the cathedral parish and leaders of the community.

I then became more aware of the importance of higher education among our Hispanic people. A good number of our parishioners had had the opportunity to receive a college education, and they now formed the nucleus of leadership in the community. I recall joining them in their efforts to encourage and support H. B. Gonzalez, then one of our parish leaders, in launching his bid for the U.S. Congress. He was eventually elected and held that post until his retirement.

The League of United Latin American Citizens (LULAC), the G.I. Forum, and the Optimist Club of San Antonio were all groups of young, well-educated, and energetic Hispanics who provided leadership in the community and were of great help to me in my efforts with the less fortunate in the parish. On one occasion a benefit baseball game was arranged between LULAC and the Optimist Club. I had given the impression of being a half-decent athlete and was asked to join one of the teams. After a few days of practice I accepted the invitation to play at the Mission Stadium, the home of the San Antonio

Missions, the minor league team in the city.

    For three innings I played left field, praying that no ball would come my way. My prayers were answered! My turn at bat produced a walk. The next one at bat got a hit, which I thought I could score on since I still had pretty good speed. But as I ran toward third base I could feel my baseball stocking falling down my leg, and in pausing to lift it up I sacrificed a few seconds. Upon reaching home, I met with the catcher who greeted me with a big smile and a ball in hand. This must have been the highlight of the game because people jokingly remind me of this incident to this day.

    San Antonio is only 150 miles north of Nuevo Laredo, Mexico and a trip to the border town was always an interesting experience. But while the church law of abstinence from meat on Fridays was strictly observed in the U.S., Mexico was dispensed from its observance of this rule. Accordingly, a group of us *epicureans* would drive to the border and into Mexico so that on Friday we might legitimately enjoy *el pajaro*—a delicious quail lunch.

    A day excursion to the border was within the law, but I had a longing to visit central Mexico in Jalisco and Michoacan, where I had lived as a child. During these years, the Claretians had no official vacation days. I asked to go into Mexico but was denied permission unless I had a legitimate reason having to do with business or ministry. I was especially drawn to young people and gave them a good portion of my time, realizing that they were the future leaders of our community. It so happens that in my ministry with these kids I had developed an outstanding basketball team, so I made arrangements for a series of matches with a military school in Monterey, Nuevo Leon, Mexico—approximately 200 miles from

San Antonio. I made sure that the schedule included a day of rest, so that we could then sneak down to La Piedad and visit my old stomping grounds.

My sacramental ministry at the cathedral brought with it some interesting experiences. Hearing confessions one late Saturday evening, I peered through the curtain toward the sanctuary. A young black youth had volunteered his services and was cleaning the vigil light containers. He happened to bend over too closely to the burning candles and his hair caught fire. I rushed out of the confessional and slapped him on the head until the fire was out. Being gifted with a healthy crop of hair, he had not even noticed the conflagration, so he was a bit surprised when I struck him on the head. But of course when he realized what had happened he thanked me for my alertness.

Another infamous incident occurred when Archbishop Robert E. Lucey was celebrating the main Sunday Mass at 10 a.m. I was his chaplain standing by his side during the offertory singing. I noticed an usher coming up the aisle with the collection basket. As he genuflected, he put his left hand into the basket and drew out bills, which he kept in his left fist. I nonchalantly left my post, went down the left aisle of the church, and as the usher reached the rear of the church I quietly told him to relinquish his takings, return them to the basket, and to leave. To this day he must be wondering how I knew.

Back to Chicago
1953-1963

After three pleasant years in San Antonio, I was assigned to Our Lady of Guadalupe Parish in South Chicago as an assistant pastor to Father Pat McPolin. He was also the chaplain of the Chicago Police Department through the St. Jude League. This position took him away from the parish a good portion of time, and in his absence I was obliged to assume added responsibilities.

The Claretian American Province was established in 1902. By the year 1954 it had spread from coast to coast, including a foundation in Canada, and had sufficient personnel to administer the various apostolic centers throughout the country. The Claretian administration in Rome, in consultation with the American Claretians, decided the U.S. field of activities should be divided into two administrations. This would provide a greater incentive for our development. The Mississippi River was to be the point of division. All states east of the Mississippi would be in the Eastern Vice Province. A new vice provincial was appointed for the area and was followed by a readjustment of personnel. McPolin was appointed superior of St. Jude Seminary, and I was appointed pastor of Our Lady of Guadalupe. I explained to the vice provincial that I did not feel competent enough to accept this responsibility. But he informed me that an older man would be appointed superior of the religious community and be stationed at Guadalupe. He promised this would lessen the pressure on me, so I accepted.

But from the very beginning it was evident that a clash would occur. We were two different personalities having two different approaches on authority and mission, and so I continued doing what I thought had to be done. The former pastor had initiated a remodeling program, and the old Cordimarian convent was absorbed as part of the rectory. I followed the plan and included a decent living room for the priests, plus a library and additional living quarters on the second floor. I thought the church built in 1928 lacked a devotional touch. The windows were too plain. So, after adequate research, I decided to install stained glass windows depicting the apparitions of Our Lady of Guadalupe. I presented the design to a company and had the windows made in Germany. People responded to the idea and contributed generously to this fund-raising program.

I felt the responsibility to participate in the area's discussion for urban renewal and better housing. To this end, I called for various meetings of the community, which occasionally were held in our parish hall. The superior, an elderly man, would sometimes show up at 9 p.m. and dismiss the people, telling them, "This is a religious community and we must be in bed by 9 p.m." I had reported these incidents to the provincial who simply remarked that the superior was the authority in a religious community. This conflict finally came to a head when on a Friday evening an assistant pastor who organized a social for the young people in the parish came to my office. He told me the superior had come to the hall and ordered all the teenagers to leave. I told the young priest I would go down to help, as he had planned to close the gatherings with a raffle. When I was on the stage speaking to the young people, the superior yanked the microphone out of my hand and ordered all the kids out. Speaking to me he shouted, "And you, Lopez, are the greatest offender!" I gently shoved him to the side of the stage, away from view of the teens, and argued that his behavior was uncalled for and that I would not stand for his attitude.

Two days later I received a call from a priest friend stationed at St. Francis, the parish where the vice provincial lived. He informed me that a note had been placed on the bulletin board announcing that a member of his community had been appointed pastor of Our Lady of Guadalupe and that I had been transferred to St. Francis. I had certainly not been informed of this change, so I called the provincial on the phone to complain of his procedure. I said that to condemn me without even listening to the circumstances was an injustice and that I would not accept his decision. I'd known in the past that relations between our vice provincial and me were strained, and I wondered if perhaps he might still have some dislike for me.

Then I spoke to the provincial of the Western province, a very understanding man with whom I had worked in San Antonio. My plans were to transfer to the Western province and my friend from the Western province recommended I write to the Claretian superior general, the head of the international

Claretian religious order, about this. But instead I swallowed my pride and, after making sure that all the parish books were in order, I quietly went to St. Francis.

I was tremendously discouraged during this year, not simply because of what I had experienced, but because I saw a pattern dating back to seminary days—a pattern I saw as destructive and dehumanizing. Some of the old-timers were still in authority, and I doubted very much that I could go along with their system. I made novena after novena to my patroness, St. Therese the Little Flower, and asked her to show me the way or to show me a sign indicating what to do.

That sign came one afternoon after a workout in our gym. I was in the shower room, which was adjacent to the provincial's office. Without straining an ear, I overheard a conversation between the provincial and one of his consultors. They were discussing possible changes of personnel for June, and were mentioning names. My name came up, and the provincial said, "I feel that I've been a bit unfair to him. Let's appoint him as pastor of Immaculate Heart of Mary Parish." So in June 1957 I moved to 45th Street and Ashland Avenue in the Back of the Yards neighborhood of Chicago.

The building was a former saloon transformed into a rectory with very simple quarters. Two Masses were celebrated each Sunday. The religious education for children drew a decent number of students. The Holy Name Society for men and the *Guadalupanas* for women kept good things happening. All in all, it was a warm community. The church itself was a hall transformed into a worship center, and again, as with Our Lady of Guadalupe, I felt it lacked the essential elements of a house of worship. With the help of carpenters from the parish and the local firemen, we designed a program of reconstruction. I went to the archdiocesan chancellor, who approved the plans, telling me, "Father, if you have the money, go ahead." The building was transformed to what it is now—a small, but beautiful *capilla*. The rectory was also given a face-lift and made a bit more comfortable and accessible.

In the meantime, on Father's Day 1959, my father died. For years he had directed a group of young parishioners who presented theatrical performances on stage at the church hall. They were scheduled to present a play that day but not everyone showed up at the designated time and place, and my father became a bit perturbed. Sometime after the late start of the play, he had a stroke and died, a short distance from the image of Our Lady of Guadalupe, whom he loved so much. Moments later, as I viewed his lifeless body, I prayed for the repose of his soul and thanked God for the family values my father had instilled in me: a respect for learning, hard work, responsibility, and a mutual caring and concern for others.

In regard to the renovations at the parish, the Claretian provincial seemed a bit displeased. Though he admired the work we had done, he was upset that it was done without his approval. I informed him that as pastor I had gone to the chancery and received the required permission, but he insisted I needed his word as well. I made the mistake of telling him that if he did not approve of my work, all he had to do was to remove me—and so he did! After three years I was on my way to Perth Amboy, New Jersey.

The initial arrival of the Claretians at Perth Amboy was not only an answer to a much-needed ministry, but I believe it was fashioned by divine providence. The order had long considered the idea of establishing a house where the Claretians arriving from Europe could stay and become acquainted with the country prior to launching out into the vast American province. After the *bracero* ministry we had left New Jersey, but Father Roy Tort, who had an instinct for being in the right place at the right time, returned to the Perth Amboy area because he saw the possibility of establishing a center where we could provide ministry to a few Portuguese families. Tort, a Claretian who had been serving in California, moved into a two-story home on Lawrence Avenue, converted the living room into a chapel, and with the bishop's approval invited the neighboring Portuguese to Sunday Mass. The Claretians have since built a large church and it presently serves as a place of worship for thousands of Puerto Rican and Dominican immigrants.

When I arrived at Perth Amboy in 1960, Fatima Chapel on Lawrence Avenue was only in its initial stage, Father Walter Mischke was pastor and limited his ministry to parishioners in the local area. Father Anibal Coehlo, a Portuguese Claretian, had just joined the staff. He had been reaching out to the Puerto Rican community in a church building formerly used to serve Hungarian Catholics. I had been designated to serve the needs of a mission in the Jackson Township 30 miles away. This meant rising early on Sunday morning and heading out to the mission for a 9 a.m. Mass in English and an 11 a.m. Mass in Spanish. I also thought it was important to add time for Confessions on Saturday afternoon, and so a fine Irish family offered me lodging on Saturday evenings to avoid the inconvenience of the drive back to Perth Amboy. Eventually the ministry in Jackson demanded a greater presence, so an extension was built on to the sacristy allowing room for a desk and a rollaway bed and a more convenient overnight stay.

The setup in Perth Amboy was only temporary, though,

since the city had plans to build a highway leading to the Outer Bridge Crossing onto Staten Island. This highway would mean our current location would be demolished, and our presence in the Garden State at this point became very unstable. I was very perturbed by the whole operation. About this same time, my mother, who had suffered from high blood pressure and diabetes, passed away. It was just 13 months after my father's death, and it affected me greatly because she was the one who had shaped my faith and my trust in God. I had been separated from her at age 13, but she had been with me each day throughout the years as I recited the morning and evening prayers she had taught me as a child: *Gracias te doy gran Senor y alabo tu gran poder, porque con el alma en el cuerpo me has dejado amanecer.* "I thank you, dear Lord, and admire your great power. You have allowed me to rise with body and soul at this hour."

To Mexico and back

1963-1972

After consulting with our new provincial, the first American Claretian to be appointed to this post, I transferred temporarily to Mexico with the intention of joining a missionary group of Claretians. I welcomed this opportunity to improve my Spanish-speaking skills. One of my assignments was to participate in a general mission in the city of Tapachula in the state of Guerrero, a city with a population of about 30,000. A group of 25 priests and about the same number of nuns arrived with the idea of canvassing the entire city. Each priest was given a certain amount of square blocks to sift through, validating marriages, baptizing children, and instructing others for Confirmation. The entire mission lasted five weeks.

On another occasion I went alone to preach a novena in preparation for the celebration of the patron saint of the town. Throughout this experience I was often edified to see the simple life of the pastors there and their spirit of self-denial. In several places there was no hot water and I had to shower by pulling a rope to release the water from a bucket. The meals were of the simplest fare and were comprised simply of beans and tortillas.

I had been in Mexico for a year when I decided to return to the U.S. and continue mission preaching, which I did for some period of time. This was shortly after the Second Vatican Council. After the constitutions of the council were published, I realized we had entered into a new era of the church. The theology I had learned in the seminary was almost obsolete, and the scripture had come alive. The change from Latin to the vernacular made a lot of sense to me. The liturgy was continually being improved, and I felt a need to be retooled, too, so I decided to take courses in theology and scripture at the University of Notre Dame for two summers.

After this experience I was again appointed to Our Lady of Guadalupe in 1964, this time with a different frame of mind. I took on the responsibility of pastor in this inner-city parish for a second time. This was during the Vietnam War, and it was my belief that many of our armed forces were being sacrificed in a meaningless struggle. I became tinged with a bit of militancy, which occasionally surfaced. The *Chicano* movement among the Hispanics, originating in the western U.S., finally affected a good number of our youth in Chicago. Chicanoism represented a new sense of pride, a new attitude, and a new awareness. The movement, however, took on an anticlerical expression and on one occasion after Mass a group of parishioners who joined the movement were demonstrating outside the church. They were shouting slogans like "Down with the church!" I understood their feelings and explained to the crowds on the street the reason for their anger. The church of Mexico in past years had sided with the rich land owners, and had certainly made many mistakes, but the church at present had made an option for the poor. I won them back to the fold and things remained peaceful for a while. We soon built a monument to the many young people of our parish who died in the Korean and Vietnam struggles. This monument still stands in the church's parking lot.

    During this time I was appointed to the provincial council as director of the apostolate for the Claretian province. My specific work was to develop and make suggestions for ministry that we were conducting in the province. I was obliged as a consultor to attend the meetings of the council and participate in the decision-making process. I was able to handle both responsibilities for some time, but soon the demands of an inner-city parish, the back surgery I had undergone, and a confrontation with a priest whose questionable sexual conduct caused damage in the community, began to take its toll. I was burnt out, and I asked for a sabbatical.

Shifting around
1972-1974

In September of 1972 I was relieved of my responsibilities as pastor and entered a sabbatical program geared toward religious priests and nuns at the University of Notre Dame. This program was introduced by the well-known Chicago social activist Father Jack Egan. The great part about the program was that we could audit any class we might be interested in. And I was even able to see a few football games that included my favorite football team—the Fighting Irish—when they played at home.

I noticed liberation theology was on the curriculum and so I decided to attend. The teacher, a former missionary in Africa, was simply narrating his experiences in the mission field and was neglecting to explain what this term *liberation* actually meant, so I didn't continue with the class, but the readings and discussions recommended by the sabbatical program were useful and interesting. But I was only three months into the sabbatical program when the provincial asked me to accept the office of treasurer in the province. The

Claretian priest who had performed this service for the past 10 years had decided to leave the order as well as the priesthood.

This meant the end of my sabbatical and a return to active duty. Our provincial house was in Oak Park, Illinois, but the administration office for the treasurer was on Madison Street in downtown Chicago. Father Joaquin De Prada had years earlier reorganized the Claretian Enterprises at the main headquarters and assigned Robert E. Burns to manage most of our activities there. He was a great help to me in explaining the ramifications of my job. I realized then that further training would be required for me to understand the language of investments and the like, so I returned to Notre Dame to take courses in the business school. I dutifully performed my responsibilities as treasurer but still longed to be involved on a pastoral level with common folk.

Through a contact with Colonel Jack Riley, Mayor Richard J. Daley's right hand man, I was appointed as one of the five city commissioners for human relations. While being careful not to neglect my responsibilities to the order, I welcomed the opportunity for involvement in the life of the City of Chicago.

The opening of new windows in the church by Pope John XXIII and the Second Vatican Council also opened many doors through which a good number of our priests began to leave. Many were rethinking their vocation to the priesthood. By 1974 some 10 young and highly qualified men had left the Claretians, and the acting provincial made it public that he, too, intended to leave when his term of office expired.

In June a chapter of elections was held in the province, and a new provincial was chosen. I was re-elected to the post of treasurer. The preceding summer I had registered for a master's degree progam at Notre Dame in business administration. I continued in the program for a second summer, driving back to Oak Park on weekends. On those long drives back and forth from Notre Dame, I began to wonder whether I had made a mistake, given that so many qualified men, including the provincial whom I admired tremendously, decided to leave the priesthood. The memory of struggles I endured while at the seminary and others I later encountered haunted me. The men who had left the priesthood were smart and highly qualified—was I making a mistake by continuing this way of life? I had left home at only 13 years of age and had not really experienced life. I wondered if I should continue in this vacuum. I realize looking back now that during those trying days I should have gone to a spiritual director, but I had been so turned off by the inadequacy and pietistic approach at the seminary that I had ruled it out.

On my own I decided to ask for a leave of absence, a time to pray, observe, and experience life outside the Claretian community. In 1974 I completed my studies at Notre Dame and entered into a training program in the Chicago Police Department. The city was about to introduce a new wrinkle in the law enforcement division, known as the Office of Professional Standards, (OPS). It would consist of a corps of qualified people hired to investigate complaints filed by citizens against individual officers who had allegedly used excessive force, engaged in corruption, or improperly used arms. I had received information about this plan as a commissioner of human relations. At a later time I attended a thorough and meaningful training program but still had not made a definite decision. A Chicago newspaper printed the list of all who had been approved for this program, and my name was on the list. I then decided to inform the provincial of my plans.

Dark night of the soul

1974-1977

The required permission for my leave was granted by our general in Rome and I began my time off in August 1974. A leave of absence simply means that I was not required to live in community as a Claretian nor would I be bound by all the restrictions of community life. I was still a priest and still a Claretian. I had taken a giant step, but it was not to be the final one. I prayed for God to grant me light and understanding, to see his will, and to understand the way I should proceed for my future. el poche syndrome had once again disrupted my life.

For over 40 years I had lived in a religious community supported by a feeling of security. At times perhaps I was disgusted with the odd behavior and strange personalities, but it had been my home and my family for the better part of my life. I was now leaving that safe haven and launching out into untested waters. It was all very scary, but at the age of 50-plus it was the decision I had arrived at.

Reality soon set in as I set out to look for living quarters and obtain necessary items to perform my job. Since I would be employed by the City of Chicago, I would have to live within its boundaries, so looking for an apartment was in and of itself an experience. Once settled in my Spartan apartment I gave myself time to reflect: Like the Israelites on their way to the Promised Land, I must not look back and remember or long for the flesh pots of Egypt; nor was I headed toward the Promised Land but to a land of Promise, a period of time to help me decide. Consequently, I would face each challenge as it was presented. The challenge at that moment was the employment to which I had committed myself: an investigator for the OPS.

This work was around the clock, coinciding with the three shifts of police officers. We were to process the complaints registered by citizens. After studying the cases, we would interview the complainant, the witnesses, and the officers. If necessary, we also went to the location where the infraction allegedly occurred. When the whole process was satisfactorily studied, analyzed, and concluded, we were able to arrive at a decision, declaring the complaint either unfounded, having insufficient evidence, or sustained. We would then submit these findings to our supervisor.

Part of the training we had undergone included a ride-along with the police officers on the midnight shift. We learned to appreciate the pressures encountered by those in law enforcement. Around the clock we had unmarked police vehicles available for the performance of our duty, and I was soon engrossed in the responsibilities of my new job.

An old saying came to mind about this time: "You can take a boy out of the country but you cannot take the country out of the boy." In my case it was: "You can take Sevy out of the priesthood, but you cannot take the priesthood out of Sevy!" As I interviewed the officers about their alleged violations, I found that a good number of them would return for friendly counseling. Many of them had known me as their pastor and felt at ease as we spoke, although they were a bit surprised to see me in a new role. Occasionally, internal affairs would call me for an opinion on certain cases, especially when alleged corruption was a concern. After working for a year as an investigator, I was given the rank of supervisor. But I soon discovered that working for the city and working for God did not necessarily go hand-in-hand. As a priest and as a Hispanic, I had developed a serious work ethic and tried to apply this practice as supervisor, demanding of my investigators the honest use of their time. I guess that was the wrong approach to use with city workers, as I was almost laughed out of my office. But some of them were conscientious workers, and we became great friends. I built up new friendships with both men and women. They all knew my position and respected it. I attended their parties, but again felt uneasy—it was that old el poche syndrome making me doubt whether I really belonged there.

    I began to appreciate some aspects of this leave of absence. On my days off from work I could really relax, a luxury I never had while in full ministry as a priest. As priests we quite often become victims of the heresy of action, feeling we must always be "on the go for Jesus." But now I could simply sit out on the shores of Lake Michigan, feel the quiet breeze, take a stroll out to Lincoln Park Zoo, or spend some quality time under the dome at the Adler Planetarium. On a Sunday morning I would pick a different parish in Chicago and attend Mass. I could have written a book on the poor quality of preaching in many a Catholic Church. And the thought came to me: No wonder so many Catholics don't attend Mass anymore! On one occasion the pastor did not even touch on the gospel theme but, ranting and raving, talked about the parking lot and how kids leave their bicycles lying all over the place. I decided then that, if and when I returned to preaching, I would not burden my audience with such unprofessional homilies unrelated to the gospel message.

All this time I kept in touch with a good number of my confreres and made an occasional visit to my provincial. On one occasion he recommended that I visit a psychiatrist friend of his for an interview that might prove helpful. I agreed. His analysis showed no pathology and his life style assessment concluded with the following:

> The vocation to the priesthood [for Severino] opened the way for him to continue his life of goodness, scholarship, and devotion, but it blocked the way leading openly and publicly to the life of affection, warmth, and sexual exuberance which his father's example had dignified for him. At the threshold of adolescence, he cast his lot on a course of action, which, as he was unable to see at the time, would lead him into fatal contradiction with his deepest ambitions, and his most dearly cherished goals.

The psychiatrist made no recommendations but had placed me face-to-face with my ambiguity. My work would now be to find out what caused it—could it be a lack of integrity?

A flashback to Bishop Fulton Sheen's television program reminded me of his observation to this effect: "If people do not live the way they think they should, they soon begin to think the way they live."

Richard J. Gilmartin, in a pamphlet called "Living Celibacy with Integrity," includes the above quote from Sheen and follows it with three proposals for the definition of *integrity*:

First, an adherence to a code of behavior.

I understood that and tried my best to observe my three vows to poverty, chastity, and obedience.

Second, to be unimpaired, to be outwardly and inwardly the same, and to live without a hidden agenda.

In spite of my human frailty, I tried to fulfill this definition.

And third, to coincide with a sense of "completeness," the condition of having no parts or elements left wanting.

With this third definition, I felt I had hit the mark! So many things were happening, or had happened, in my life as a priest that caused me to feel incomplete. Yes, I had worked hard—both as an assistant pastor and as a pastor. I had exercised the office of treasurer with care, but little by little a feeling of self-satisfaction and self-service began to crawl in. Perhaps I was motivated by the desire to be recognized or to look good, or simply to please others.

During this period of my leave of absence, I also attended symposia for priests who were in similar states of limbo. There were interesting discussions on balance, perspective, and relationships. In one of these sessions, the director candidly stressed the importance of good life-giving relationships. Gilmartin had also written about a fellow priest who had a close friendship with a married woman who had children. They shared that his celibacy meant a lot to her and to him as well. Theirs was a life-giving relationship, and he believed that because of this friendship he was a better priest. Another observation the director of the symposium made, was that the Catholic priesthood requiring celibacy, or a life without sex, does not necessarily preclude warm friendships and intimate relationships. All of this, of course, made sense, and it was certainly different from the Jansenistic inhibitions imposed on us by some of our directors in the early years of seminary training.

    I was now in the third year of my leave of absence, and I was beginning to reconstruct my outlook and establish a good basis for making a decision about my vocation. Around that time my older brother, Robert, whom I greatly admired, died of heart failure. He had been very disappointed when I began my leave of absence, but when I explained my reasons to him he was supportive. Shortly after Robert's death I was hospitalized myself and underwent a laminectomy. While in the hospital recovering from this back surgery, I mused, looking back at the last three years, that to an extent they had been years of grace. God had allowed his grace to slowly seep through the hard clay that my life had become.

    Sometime ago I came across these words written by the theologian Paul Tillich. They reveal the exact message God was giving to me those days in the hospital. It reads as follows:

> *Grace strikes us when we are in great pain and restlessness. It strikes us when we walk through the dark valley of a meaningless and empty life. It strikes when we feel our separation is deeper than usual. It strikes when disgust for our own being, for our own indifference, our weakness, our hostility, and our lack of direction and composure have become intolerable. It strikes us when, year after*

year, the longed for perfection of life does not appear, when old compulsions reign within us, as they have for decades, when despair destroys all joy and courage. Sometimes, at that moment, a wave of light breaks into our darkness, and it is as though a voice were saying: "You are accepted, accepted by that which is greater than you, and the name of which you do not know. Do not try to do anything now, perhaps later you will do much. Do not seek for anything, do not perform anything. Do not intend anything, simply accept the fact that you are accepted."

This was my turning point. God's grace had once again led me to realize that I was a full-fledged child of his and the path he had placed me on at age 13 was truly the one to follow. I knew then I had finally overcome this el poche syndrome and ended my leave of absence for a return to a full sacerdotal ministry.

Back on track
1977-1984

The provincial superior came to visit me at the hospital, and I informed him then of my decision. I also informed the director of OPS, and we set August 31, 1977 as the final date for my term as supervisor for the Office of Professional Standards in Chicago's police department.

A warm send-off by the OPS—including the official retirement of my star, which was presented to me in a decorated frame—made me once again available for full-time ministry. Though still a bit weak physically, I felt spiritually strong and anxious for priestly work. A request had been made to our provincial for a campus minister to minority students at the University of Illinois in Champaign. I visited the campus and obtained detailed information but decided not to accept the post. At this stage in my life I knew I needed a supportive community, and I felt this position would have isolated me from the order.

The right opportunity came, though, offering me a similar

ministry at George Mason University in northern Virginia. The Claretians had for many years supplied a priest for campus ministry at this university, at the request of the local bishop. I accepted this offer, since I would be living with the Claretians at St. Mary of Sorrows Rectory in Fairfax Station, just a short drive from the university. The Claretian staff was very supportive and welcoming.

Campus ministry occupied most of my time, but on weekends I would help by celebrating Mass and participating in parish activities. I had a bit of extra time on my hands, though, so I enrolled in a master's degree program in Spanish literature. All went well the first year. The next year, however, the order requested that I go to Rome to provide instantaneous translations at the general chapter convening in the Eternal City. Consequently, I was unable to comply with all the requirements of the master's program and was obliged to resume it later upon my return.

George Mason University had grown tremendously during those few years that I was gone. No longer was it a small college in northern Virginia but a well-known and respected university providing students the highest quality education. I served as campus minister for four years. In 1981, Father RIchard Farrell, who had been the pastor of St. Mary's since 1969, asked to be relieved of his position and accepted another as head of a parish in Missouri. I was then appointed pastor of St. Mary's—this small, historic church built in 1858, during the Civil War. It had once served as the hospital where Clara Barton, who organized the American Red Cross, rendered service to the wounded soldiers.

St. Mary's had been a small rural church with 175 families at the arrival of the Claretians in 1969, but was now a suburban parish with close to 3,000 families. It was quite a challenge to be a pastor of this completely Anglo-Saxon faith community. I had been pastor of a number of Hispanic parishes where we struggled to make ends meet, but here a good number of CIA, FBI, and many other government employees considered St. Mary of Sorrows their church. Here I was, a Mexican American Claretian, requested to serve, minister, and preach, to these high-powered citizens. It was scary, and the old el poche syndrome was again rearing its ugly head. But after reading the history of this church I remembered that a Mexican priest by the name of Valentino Cuevas had been the first full-time pastor of St. Mary's in 1918—the year I was born. A thought entered my mind: This parish had waited long enough for another Mexican American priest! And with confidence and trust in God I would accept this challenge.

I soon discovered that in their work of 13 years, the Claretians had molded the people into a vibrant and caring faith community. So I went along with the pastoral plan. The various committees covered every conceivable area of parish life. Their interest and concern went beyond parish limits. The social action committee encouraged involvement with the needs of the poor in other countries as well as locally. At the recommendation of the diocese, our parish adopted a newly-arrived Vietnamese family and for three years assisted them in every way until they were on their feet. We also adopted three Cuban prisoners released by Fidel Castro and helped them through the difficult process of their readjustment to life here.

Though St. Mary's was a completely English-speaking parish, it reached out to the Spanish-speaking immigrants that were beginning to settle in Fairfax County. Religious and social activities were initiated among them under the direction of Pilar Soto Kotwicki. We even adopted a poor parish in Guatemala as our "sister parish." But we still had to meet and solve the local needs. We built a new parish center, but with it came a large debt. The interest payments on the loan were exorbitant, as the interest had risen to an all-time high of 21 percent, but by the end of three years our debt was almost nonexistent and the mortgage was liquidated.

A touch of mission work and Casa Claret

1984-1990

In one of our province assemblies an idea came up to establish a program among the Hispanic youth to motivate them toward higher education. This program would also be an opportunity to discern vocations. The provincial remembered my interest and was giving serious thought to this program. Consequently, after three years as pastor of St Mary's, I was asked to transfer back to Chicago and work on the preliminaries of this venture. But this plan had to be put aside for a while because of an emergency stiuation. One of our missionaries in Guatemala became seriously ill, and I was asked to fill in during his illness. Soon afterwards, I was on my way to Guatemala and anxious to get my feet wet in a mission ministry.

The Claretians had accepted the invitation to establish a mission in Guatemala in 1965. A large area in the northeast section of the country known as Izabal was recommended by the bishop as a fertile mission field. This area included indigenous villages in the mountains, jungles, and *Ladino* (persons of mixed Guatemalan and Indian heritage) settlements along the shores of Lake Izabal. By the year 1984, when I arrived, the mission had greatly developed, having four centers where native catechists could receive adequate training. The missionaries could then return to these centers after their long trips through mountain villages, celebrating the Eucharist and administering various sacraments. Two trade schools had been opened and were functioning well, giving the Q'eqchi Indian youth an opportunity for a better education.

I had visited these centers in earlier years, in my role as treasurer of the province, to assess the needs of our men. My work with the mission would now allow me to share in their ministry. I went into the mountain villages and, with a catechist as a guide, celebrated the Eucharist, visited the sick, and spent quality time with the Q'eqchi people. The catechists were invaluable, as they translated my every word. The other padres in the mission were fluent in the Q'eqchi language, but all I could say was "hello" and "good-bye," which they seemed to appreciate. I always marveled at their hospitality and sincerity. They lived on simple dirt floor huts, yet they were immaculately clean!

The ministry of our men in Guatemala was not always unhampered, nor performed in an atmosphere of tranquility. Some landowners looked askance at the land the Indians occupied and were anxious to possess it. They often made use of the Guatemalan army as a tool in their nefarious purpose to take the Indians' land. The missionaries who came to the defense of the Indians proved an obstacle to these wrongdoers, and they harassed and threatened the missionaries.

A young padre from the Claretian English province by the

name of Chris Newman had joined the intial group of missionaries who had arrived in 1966. He soon became quite active among the Q'eqchi. He had mastered their language and spent most of his time visiting the aldeas and the villages in the innermost part of the mountaineous region. In his efforts to build up a local church community, he defended the indigenous people's right to their land and drew the anger of the wealthy landowners. He became a particular target of the landowners.

Seven of the catechists trained by the Claretians were killed, and when two of Newman's catechists met the same fate it was discovered that part of the killers' plot was also to murder Father Newman. Newman had not been with the catechists at the time of the incident, and so narrowly escaped. As a result, the mission team recommended he return to England for his own safety. He has recently returned to Central America to serve the Claretian mission team in Belize.

The mission center where I stayed during this period was Santo Tomás, a port in the Caribbean a short distance from a Guatemalan army post. The captain of that post was also the head of the Port Authority. He had asked me if I would say Mass at the camp on Sunday. I said I would be happy to do so, provided he would listen to one complaint. Then I explained the purpose of our mission and the harassment we were experiencing from the army, especially in the Rio Dulce area where we had recently opened a center. I'm not sure whether the captain responded agreeably to me because I was frank and honest or because I was a Mexican-American—a strange breed he had never encountered. But regardless of his reasons I was assured that, at least in his area, the harassment would stop. A week later I accompanied one of our men—another young, English padre who had recently been assigned to the Rio Dulce post. He was a bit uneasy as we drove to our destination. But when we did encounter some soldiers on the road, they simply waved at us. I breathed a sigh of relief, blessed myself, and we confidently went on our way.

I had the opportunity of visiting other mission centers and marveled at their development. Father Tom Moran, who had spent about 20 years in these missions, had developed El Estor into a vital community with a trade school, supervised by the De La Salle brothers. Livingston mission, on the Caribbean coast where Father Anthony Briskey had dedicated a good portion of his life, was now thriving as well. Father Richard Todd had built the physical plant at Santo Tomás, and it became the center where all the missionaries would gather for the training of their respective catechists.

But after nine months in that picturesque area of Guatemala, I returned to Chicago, anxious to tackle a new project.

The following paragraph is taken from a booklet printed in 1952 to commemorate the 50th anniversary of the Claretians' arrival in the United States:

From Austin, the capital of Texas, to the Mexican border there wasn't a Mexican settlement, as small as it might be, where the influence of the Claretians was not felt. They preached, administered the sacraments, and instructed the children, often under the shadow of a tree, in a little hut, or in a poor dwelling.

The Claretians had been invited by American bishops to help preserve the light of faith among the Spanish-speaking Catholics in this country. As we settled and established parishes, the importance of education was seriously considered. Our early fathers made sure every parish under their supervision had a parochial school. In fact, three high schools were built by the order in a short period of time after their arrival. Presently, in spite of many school closings in Chicago, two parochial schools in Claretian parishes are thriving with capacity attendance in each school.

This success, and special interest in education in the past, prompted our Claretian Eastern province to consider the ways and means to assist and energize Hispanic youth in the Chicago area toward a higher education. At Our Lady of Guadalupe Church in South Chicago we had been successful in convincing our parochial school graduates to finish high school. A few who qualified for college took our advice and accepted that challenge. The great majority would, however, opt for the local mills. The pay was good, but these jobs offered no security. All the mills eventually shut down, and these men, having no other skills, found it difficult to obtain other employment. The memory of these unpleasant situations prompted me to join in the effort to energize our Hispanic youth to be dedicated to their education.

The plan was to establish a center, open it to prospective students to live in community and in an environment conducive to study. They would have a side job, and two priests were assigned to encourage and direct them. The responsibility to find an adequate location for the center was given to me and to Bruce Wellems, who was not yet ordained but was finishing his studies at the Chicago Theological Union (CTU). We combed the city of Chicago from the North Side to the South, looking for a convent that had been vacated. We eventually opted for a building next to St. Attracta Church in

Cicero for the ideal spot. The students would be involved in the liturgy of the parish, and transportation to the various universities was convenient. Our first efforts were rewarded when a group of eight students responded. The project got underway and in September 1985 we moved into the building, calling the project Casa Claret. Wellems was ordained to the priesthood in January 1986 and became the taskmaster for the project. As the senior padre in residence, I simply supported him.

We avoided a seminary-like approach to the project with less regimentation, and counseling was available. We all, including the priests, took our turn in preparing the meals, shopping, and keeping the house in order. The students were obliged to take on a side job, which would not interfere with their school or study period, and also to be involved in a community project. The program worked well for three years at St. Attracta in Cicero, but because of a lack of adequate space and other complications, we were obliged to look elsewhere in order to further develop the program. Our quest led us to Chicago's inner city, a section known as, the "Heart of Chicago." The convent across the street from St. Paul's Church and parochial school had been recently vacated. It was a three-story building with ample room. The pastor, Father Phil Guerin, was willing to allow us to move in, provided—as he explained—that we take over the whole parish! He further explained that he was about to retire and that the archdiocese did not have anyone to replace him. The topic was brought to our provincial assembly, and, after consulting with the archdiocese, the Claretian Eastern province agreed, on a probationary basis, to accept St. Paul's Parish as one of its corporate ministries.

So in August 1987 the Casa Claret project moved into the St. Paul convent. Two years later, we celebrated the graduation of five of the original class of eight who had come into the program. They graduated from De Paul University, Loyola University, and the University of Illinois in Chicago. Today one of them is a doctor and two are certified public accountants. When initially started, Casa Claret was a four-year experiment—if it wasn't successful, it would be terminated. The program continues to this date, but under a different administration. And though not as successful as anticipated, it is still available.

With the transfer of Casa Claret to St. Paul's convent, I was appointed future pastor of St. Paul, to replace Father Guerin upon his retirement. I moved into the rectory in August and took on the ministry of assisting him until his retirement in January 1988. St Paul's was built by German immigrants 100 years earlier. It is an architectural gem and is mentioned in the *Guinness Book of Records* as "the church built without a nail." Its spires are the tallest in Chicago and are visible in Chicago's skyline for miles. Its building and grounds have often been used in the filming of movies.

The parish experienced gradual changes. Only a few families have remained from its original German membership, and it is now predominantly Mexican. In taking full responsibility as pastor, my task was not only to provide a ministry to those attending the parish but also to energize many neighborhood families who were traveling to other parishes where adequate liturgies in Spanish were provided. The former pastor, though able to speak Spanish, was in poor health and the parish had been understaffed. With the help of Wellems and the Casa Claret boys across the street we initiated a program to revitalize the neighborhood. We made friendly visits to parishioners' homes that would include Masses and at times an Anointing.

On one occasion, I was summoned to a house where a young lady was sick and had been acting a bit strange. I was told that she seemed to be possessed by the devil. I certainly did not know what to expect, so I took my holy oils for Anointing the Sick, a crucifix, and some holy water. I entered the home and approached the bed where the young lady was lying. She lifted up her head and seemed to levitate about two feet from her bed! She cursed and then spat at me!

I kept my distance, not knowing what to expect from her next, much less what I should do next. On former occasions I had been asked to bless apartments or homes where residents claimed they heard strange noises, presumably caused by *esperantos*, or ghosts. At these times, I generally sprinkled the premises with holy water and invited the occupants to pray with me for protection. I tried to assure them tranquility by pointing out various physical conditions of the building which were likely to cause such noises. But this was an entirely different situation.

I had never seen such a strange phenomenon in all my life. I knew that the church in ages past had instituted the practice of exorcism which could only be evoked in extraordinary cases and required the approval of the local bishop. I was also aware that the situation I was facing could be the result of a psychological aberration and not exactly a diabolical possession, so I asked the family to join me in prayer. I instructed them to keep an eye on her and call me if they thought my presence was needed again.

Upon returning to the rectory, I breathed a deep sigh of

relief, thanking God for delivering me from such an ordeal as pictured in the popular thriller *The Exorcist*. I kept in touch with the family, who informed me that she had eventually regained her health and was now living a normal life.

St. Paul's church had a large choir loft, and a huge pipe organ that many years earlier had been brought from Germany but had not been used. Inquiring from experts into the possibility of restoring it to use, I was informed that the cost was prohibitive and in this day and age virtually impossible. Fortunately for us, Wellems, his brother, and sister-in-law were all accomplished musicians and made up for the lack of having a good organ. They organized a splendid choir in the parish and contributed to meaningful liturgies on Sundays. St. Paul's School, with its full enrollment each year, benefited from the neighboring presence of Casa Claret students, who helped with the tutoring program.

My term as pastor of St. Paul's was a bittersweet experience, though. On the one hand, as a Mexican American padre, I couldn't have asked for a better location. The densely populated neighborhood was mostly Mexican and a good portion of the immigrants were from my homeland states of Jalisco and Michoacan. Their mannerisms, *dichos*, idiomatic expressions, idiosyncrasies, and their particular culture made me feel at home. When they spoke about Atotonilco, Los Altos, or La Piedad, we had something in common.

I felt at ease, too, at nearby Benito Juarez High School where a great majority of the students were Mexican American. The principal would occasionally contact me when a student would stray from the path, and I would respond by visiting the home and having a family meeting to discuss the matter. In addition, both the alderman and the committeeman from the ward were Mexican Americans who listened to recommendations for the betterment of the community. I also saw the opening of the first Mexican Art Museum in Chicago, just a few blocks from our church, as well as the transformation of Cermak Road, which bisected the neighborhood, into a Mecca of Mexican businesses featuring everything from tortillerias and taquerias to *tienda de abarrotes* grocery stores. I could walk through these stores demystified and in plain clothes, and people would greet me with "Buenos días, Padre!" Mine was a high-demand, low-reward ministry, but the reward came with the people's response to the many activities we offered or with a simple invitation to share their *chilaquiles* at *su humilde casa* (their humble home).

 A 100-year-old building sooner or later begins to show its age, though, and St. Paul's was no exception. The roof leaked and the walls were badly in need of tuck-pointing. Even the pigeons abandoned the tallest steeples in the city that used to be their landing pads. The building needed immediate attention. With my portfolio containing all the information, I headed to the archdiocesan office to make my report and appeal for financial assistance. I had made an appointment to speak to a deacon who was at the head of finances. He explained to me that the upkeep and repairs of buildings were the responsibility of the parish and furthermore St. Paul's had an outstanding debt due to a previous failure to liquidate assets from the archdiocese. No explanation of our limited resources would suffice. This attitude seemed strange to me, so I then attempted to make an appointment to speak to the cardinal about my situation. But my quest was in vain.

 Quite some time later, I was told that the chancellor, who is the administrative head of the diocese, had built an iron ring around the cardinal, which was difficult to get past. Sometime after I left St. Paul's the cardinal became aware of this impropriety. He removed the chancellor who eventually left the priesthood. The cardinal established direct contact with his pastors and, upon learning of St. Paul's condition, he helped generously with money for repairs.

During my tenure, however, I felt a bit frustrated. The pressures and strain of this highly demanding position eventually affected my health. I underwent heart surgery and, upon recovering, continued as pastor until the new triennial appointments were made. My one and only sabbatical had been 18 years prior, but was interrupted as I abruptly accepted the position of treasurer. Now at the age of 72, I decided to resume my plan to take that sabbatical.

Finally, sabbatical
1990

In 1990, upon making assignments for the next triennium, the provincial granted my request for a sabbatical. I chose Claret House, the Claretian house of studies, as my residence. This center is strategically located in Hyde Park, in walking distance from both the University of Chicago and CTU. Its proximity to Lake Michigan and Jackson Park's 18-hole public golf course provided much relaxation. The universities were ideal for study and research, prompting my decision to audit a psychology in ministry class at CTU. It proved beneficial for reviewing old material.

Some years earlier I had made contact with the Center of Ministry Transition in St. Louis, under the Direction of Richard Johnson. One of the purposes of this program was to introduce the elements of healthy growth into and through the renewal stage and, finally, to a healthy and fruitful retirement when that time comes. I had taken the RSPR (Retirement Success Profile for Religious) and my personal profile scores indicated I should remain active in my ministry. This sabbatical would give me an opportunity to discover and review where I stood. There were many other actions this program recommended for my consideration in order to positively prepare for retirement. This sabbatical year would allow time for me to study and pray about these recommendations.

    The sabbatical year provided me an opportunity to relax and endeavor to restore luster to my life, a luster necessary to help religious remain alive, vital, and filled with zest. During this year, my visits to the cardiologist revealed I needed a pacemaker, as my heartbeat had become relatively low. After having one implanted, walking the 18 holes at Jackson Park golf course seemed quite achievable. The Claretian community at Hyde Park, including professed students attending CTU and their priest directors, all made for a wonderfully supportive group. Bishop Wilton Gregory, a future president of the United States Catholic Conference of Bishops, occupied one of the apartments and would occasionally join us for meals. On weekends I would help out at one of our local parishes.

Back in the saddle, heading south

1991-2001

The Claretians normally have two assemblies per year, including a short gathering during the Christmas holidays and another during the summertime. The first is usually for camaraderie and to create a better community, but occasionally important matters are brought up. The summer gathering is designed for new business. The mini-assembly held during my sabbatical year decided to discuss the possibility of opening a new English-speaking ministry. The Claretians had left Fairfax, Virginia after having served St. Mary of Sorrows Parish for 22 years, a parish that the diocese was then ready to administer.

It was agreed that since personnel was available we should offer our services to dioceses in the South where the need appeared greater. This was eventually done, and various positive requests were received. Two priests were assigned to visit each of these dioceses to evaluate the need and present a report back to the Claretian community. Father Richard Farrell and I were assigned to visit Savannah,

Georgia; Charleston, South Carolina; and Atlanta. When all of these reports were discussed at the summer assembly, the request made by the archbishop of Atlanta seemed to be the most urgent, and so the Claretian Eastern province decided to accept his invitation.

Eventually, a team of four priests was assigned to the Atlanta archdiocese. I was selected to be one of the four, as Archbishop James P. Lyke indicated the number of Hispanics was increasing in his archdiocese and that the Claretians may be asked to assist in this ministry. I accepted under the condition that I would not be involved in the administration of the parish. Three other Claretians—Greg Kenny, Richard Farrell, and Wayne Schimmelman—arrived at Corpus Christi Parish in Stone Mountain, Georgia on June 15, 1992 to serve and administer the parish. I had recently undergone another back surgery and remained in Chicago to recover. I arrived at Corpus Christi on August 23, and I began to minister to the spiritual needs of the parish, specifically to the Hispanic members of the community. This ministry extended not only to those who attended Corpus Christi, but also to Hispanic parishioners of St. John Neumann in Lilburn, about 15 miles away. I would celebrate Sunday Eucharist in Stone Mountain at 11:30 a.m., then rush to St. John Neumann for a 1 p.m. Mass.

Stone Mountain, Georgia, prior to the civil rights movement in the 1960s, had been a stronghold of the Ku Klux Klan. The grand wizard, who owned a large portion of what is now called Stone Mountain Park, had established his headquarters in this seemingly sleepy southern town. It has since changed hands and is now owned by the state and leases all the concessions to the Silver Dollar City Enterprises. The carvings on the side of the mountain depict Civil War officers Gen. Robert E. Lee, Gen. "Stonewall" Jackson, and the president of the Confederacy, Jefferson Davis. The park commission recently added a structure named "Crossroads," modeled after a town set in the 1880s. But the jury is still out on whether this change has hurt or helped this beautiful setting. Stone Mountain is the most visited place in the South, second only to Disney World.

In the shadows of Stone Mountain, and a relatively short distance from the park, lies Corpus Christi Parish, established in 1971 by the Archdiocese of Atlanta. It had its humble beginnings using the local public elementary school for its Sunday liturgy. Eventually, a church, gymnasium, and rectory were built among the pine trees in an ideal, picturesque location.

The Sunday Hispanic liturgy at Corpus Christi was being celebrated in the gymnasium, but the Claretian staff thought that, for better integration of Hispanics with the whole parish, that this Mass should be celebrated in the main church. The pastor suggested I address the parishioners at all Masses to explain this change, since the 1 p.m. English Mass would be replaced by this Mass in Spanish. Most of the English-speaking applauded the change, except for a few who were set on attending at 1.

Georgia is one of the states reporting a significant increase of Hispanic immigrants in the last decades. In the 1990s the farmland states as well as the industrial ones attracted Hispanics from as far as California. They came to Georgia fleeing from the effects of Proposition 187, which limited immigrant entitlements. Trailer parks throughout the extended Atlanta area became overcrowded. Upon my arrival there were only five Hispanic priests in the Atlanta archdiocese, so the need for additional bilingual clergy became evident.

Since then the newly appointed Archbishop, John Donoghue, has arranged for Colombian priests to be incorporated into the Atlanta archdiocese, and the number of Hispanic priests has substantially increased. The influx of immigrants in Georgia, as I discovered upon my arrival, led to a love/hate situation. Many of the industries and farmlands welcomed them since there was a workforce shortage. The general public, however, convinced the Immigration and Naturalization Service to remove them from the state. Raids were conducted by the INS, and immigrant workers were arrested and deported at their places of employment without even providing them an opportunity to contact family members. Some of our Hispanic priests organized a demonstration at the INS building in Atlanta. We were not defending their illegal status but condemning the cruel and inhuman treatment by the INS.

On this occasion, I submitted the following article to *The Georgia Bulletin*, the Atlanta archdiocesan weekly newspaper:

> *We have learned of the 'raids' conducted by the departments of immigration in the Atlanta area. Many of those taken in these raids were Mexican, who had come to this country seeking work for their livelihood, the same as my parents did over 60 years ago. It seems, though, that these people are 60 years late, and presumably, that makes them illegal...*

I recall having read an article in the *Los Angeles Times* written by columnist Robert Sheer in 1993 during the controversy of Proposition 187. The writer quoted Cardinal

Roger Mahony of California:
> *Much is at stake in the way we respond to the immigrants today. We must not follow the lead of those fanning the flames of intolerance. The right to move across borders to escape political persecution, or in search of economic survival is a theme of extraordinary importance in Catholic social thinking.*

Another area of concern in Georgia was the School of the Americas in Fort Benning in Columbus. This military school was reputed to have trained military personnel from Central American countries who then returned to their country using the methods of torture they learned at SOA on their own people. Visits and organized demonstrations showing opposition to that school were included in our promotion of social justice. Our demonstrations, organized by concerned groups throughout the country, eventually produced results and caught the eye of the military.

The Olympic Games came to Atlanta in 1996. A few months prior to beginning the scheduled games the International Olympics Committee (IOC) came to the city and met with Billy Payne, the local organizer, in order to finalize the preparations for this great celebration. Upon their arrival, Juan Antonio Samaranch, the president of the IOC, informed our community that he had become aware of the Claretians' presence in the Atlanta area. He hoped that one of us might celebrate the Eucharist for his international committee during their stay in Atlanta. I volunteered and committed myself for the weekends that the games were in Atlanta. But as the games progressed I received a call from the archdiocese requesting that I discontinue this service. Rumors had reached its office questioning Mr. Samaranch's standing with the church. Having had many conversations with him, I knew those rumors to be false. I arranged an interview for Mr. Samaranch with both the archbishop and the editor of the *The Georgia Bulletin*. The matter was favorably cleared.

In October of the same year I received word that my older sister Charlotte had cancer. She and her husband had sold their home some years earlier and moved into Villa Guadalupe, a retirement center across the street from Our Lady of Guadalupe Church and the Shrine of St. Jude in South Chicago. Raul, my sister's husband, had died a year earlier, and Charlotte was now alone, but we had talked frequently and visited to keep in touch. My sister Carmen called to tell me that Charlotte's condition was critical, so I went to Chicago to be with her in her last days. Her funeral Mass was celebrated at Our Lady of Guadalupe Church. I was the celebrant and delivered the following homily:

Shortly before coming to Chicago from Atlanta, and before being informed of my sister Charlotte's death, I had an interesting conversation with a member of our parish in Stone Mountain. In the course of conversation she said, "You priests are so lucky. You live in a holy environment and are always talking about holy things."

I did not dissuade her but thought to myself: "That can be good and bad." We eventually might run into the danger of dealing with holy things so often that we take them for granted and miss out on the tremendous contents of these so-called holy things. We perform Marriages, Baptisms, hear Confessions, and from there we hurry on to other re-

sponsibilities in our life, which we believe are just as important. But perhaps we miss out on reality by not giving thought to the life-giving aspect of what we have just accomplished.

The same thing I feel can be said about our assisting in funerals. Temporarily we do give thought to the individual situation and try to bring solace to the bereaved, but then life goes on as usual and we become engaged in other mundane occupations. But then, when we personally experience the death of a close friend or relative, we pause and begin to reflect more attentively on the common denominator of humanity. Of late, death has been tapping us on the shoulder with a little stronger tap than usual.

The Claretian priests gathered about three weeks ago for the funeral of Father Marty, a relatively young man. Sometime before that we had been informed of the death of Father Grainer, a former Claretian priest whom we all knew very well. Today we are here for the exequies of my sister Charlotte, while my first cousins in California are gathered for the funeral of Mary Parra, who died on the same day as Charlotte. With all these circumstances, it is no wonder that today we give Charlotte's death special emphasis and attention.

About two weeks ago, I was here in Chicago and went to visit my sister in the hospital. The previous day she had been informed that she had cancer and that it was in a quite developed stage. She told me, "Sevy, I'm scared." Deep in my heart I knew that her fear was justified. Death is change, and change is *always fearful as well as challenging, and until we admit fear we cannot accept the challenge. I spoke to her about Cardinal Bernardin and how he, as a victim of cancer, realized it was too soon to die. I mentioned that he encouraged us to look upon death as a friend, not as an enemy. I said to her, "You know, Charlotte, you and I have lived a pretty long life, you are 84 and I'm 78.*

"Through this illness, God is telling you, 'Charlotte, you have suffered quite a bit in your life. Your life has not been a bed of roses. Oh yes, there have been pleasant moments in your life, but there have also been some real hurts. Leave everything behind and come and join me."

I didn't know what effect my words would have on Charlotte, but my sister Carmen, who was with her each day after I left, tells me that she was very resigned and peaceful.

As Christians and as Catholics, and so much more as priests, we come across so many beautiful quotations that should stir up our hope and our faith, quotations from the Word of God that we find in the Bible. We find these words in the book of Job: "Oh, I know that my Redeemer lives and that I shall see him after the corruption of my flesh."

St. Paul, in his Second Letter to the Corinthians, states: "I know that if this tent is destroyed, I have a building, not built by my hand but by the hand of God, eternal in the heavens."

St. John tells us, "I know that I am a child of God, but I still do not know what I shall be when I grow up," "I know that I shall see him as He is." "I am the resurrection and the life, whoever believes in me, though he dies, yet shall live" (John 3).

When we see Father Marty suddenly taken from our midst, when we see Charlotte, my sister, or Charlotte, your mother, departing for all eternity, these quotations take on a special meaning when we are faced with the death of someone close to us.

Now about Charlotte herself in life: When I was about 10 or 11, Charlotte thought she had a calling to become a nun and joined the Cordimarian Sisters. She spent some time with them in San Antonio, but during her novitiate became quite sick and accepted this as a sign that religious life was not her calling. Throughout her life, either as a wife or as a mother, she showed tremendous faith in God and fidelity to Christian principles.

Charlotte's Mass this morning marks the fifth member of the Lopez family at whose funeral I have assisted. Those of you who have known our family probably remember my dad who passed away in 1959, my mother in 1960, Bob in 1977, and Joe in 1989.

Somehow or another the sting of death does not feel so sharp within these walls of Guadalupe. Whether it's the architecture of the building that sort of makes you feel like God's arms are embracing you and telling you to "have no fear, I am here," or Our Lady of Guadalupe's mantel that extends to us from her place, wrapping herself around us and giving us warmth, I do not know.

It could also be the faith that the Claretian Fathers have instilled in us, in this very place from its very beginning. But something gives us hope and helps us bear the apparent ugliness of death. So as we are saddened by the separation from Charlotte, let us rejoice in the knowledge that, for her, suffering is no more, that she has joined the great crowd of those who are now enjoying the reward of their faith.

Lending a hand

since 2001

The Claretians in the U.S. are encouraged to speak both Spanish and English so that each priest can be more versatile when it comes time for the triennial changes and adjustment of personnel. An additional bilingual Claretian was assigned to Corpus Christi in 2001, giving me an opportunity to branch out not only into English ministry but also to other areas of Hispanic ministry.

Having four priests in a parish is considered a luxury in the Atlanta archdiocese. And, though my last three years at Corpus Christi have been defined as a period of "active retirement," I have certainly been more active than retired. But this has given me the freedom to assist our missionaries wherever reinforcements are needed.

Some years ago the Claretians from Mexico and our two provinces in the U.S. joined forces to establish a mission in Juarez, Mexico. The location chosen was a development in the desert, southeast of Juarez, called Tierra Nueva. Thousands of indigent people from the interior of Mexico, attracted by this supposed "promised land," flocked to the border. This development coincided with the building of the *maquiladoras*, factories and assembly plants brought there by foreign companies. Adequate housing for these thousands had not been provided, and consequently these newcomers were forced to build their own dwellings out of whatever material they could find—cardboard, discarded crates, and adobes—to become squatters in the desert land. These are the families that the Claretians decided to assist.

In February 2001, willing to lend a hand, I decided to spend all of Lent at the mission in Tierra Nueva. It was quite a revelation. Two of our Claretians had established four centers in the desert where these people had settled. I volunteered to minister at the main mission during my stay, as the other two padres made the rounds to other missions. As Holy Week drew near, the situation became quite demanding, but I was greatly edified by the lifestyle of our missionaries. For housing they had transformed a simple hall into living quarters to include a kitchen, dining area, and bathroom. A curtain and a few dressers defined the sleeping area for each of us. I was thankful for small favors, such as the fact that no one in the group snored. (I understand that now our priests there have decent living quarters, and an order of nuns has been added to the staff.) The priests made not only the Eucharist and other sacraments available, but they also became concerned with the day-to-day needs of the people. At the main mission station in Tierra Nueva, a medical dispensary was erected as well as a system of food and clothing distribution.

The Juarez Diocese had recently taken a survey, gathering information concerning the effects of the *maquiladoras* on the life of the people. Though they did bring with them opportunities for employment, their arrival also had many negative effects. The following is some of the information gathered in the survey:

> *The average salary was 60 pesos a day ($5 USD), and the work was 48 hours per week. Employees would try to work overtime in order to meet living expenses, food, shelter, clothing, etc. Workers were not allowed to unionize. Husbands and wives, while working, would often leave children unattended, and family values were gradually being destroyed.*

During my Lenten stay, I also became aware of the horrendous crimes being committed in the area—serial murders and disappearances of more than 300 young women and girls, their lifeless bodies thrown into the desert sands in the vicinity of our mission. Two of them were catechists at the mission. I witnessed a cavalcade of women dressed all in black who went from the state capital in the city of Chihuahua to Juarez—a distance of 75 miles—to protest against the government, which they believed had not moved to solve and stop these crimes. Amnesty International has since directed a campaign in an effort to transform these happenings from forgotten tragedies to international concerns and to motivate the local government to investigate this situation. This is the scene that greeted the Claretians as they reached out to this neglected area and those people in the desert, a bit south of the border and beyond Juarez.

The following year, during Lent of 2003, I offered my services to Holy Cross Church in Chicago, a parish established by Lithuanian immigrants shortly after the First World War.

They had built a magnificent church with a capacity to seat close to 1,000 worshipers. Adjacent to the church was a three-story rectory housing over a dozen Lithuanian priests who were expelled from their country during turbulent years. The neighborhood, one of the most densely populated in Chicago, is now completely Hispanic. The Archdiocese of Chicago in 1981 merged Immaculate Heart of Mary Parish with Holy Cross and asked the Claretians to administer the new arrangement.

The pastor at present is Father Bruce Wellems, who had been with me in Cicero when we established the Casa Claret. He is a man of tremendous energy and zeal who addresses the basic needs and problems of the neighborhood. Both he and an elderly colleague, Father George Ruffolo, are providing spiritual nourishment to the parish, but Father Bruce has been giving special attention to gang proliferation, a phenomenon no doubt abetted by an overwhelming number of high school dropouts. He opened an alternative high school, encouraging the gang member dropouts to return and complete their education. He also established a fund for college scholarships and was supported in this project not only by local businesspeople and friends of the Claretian province but also by Cardinal Francis George and the mayor of Chicago, Richard M. Daley.

While at Holy Cross, and during the Lenten season, I was able to lighten the burden of our men in their sacramental ministry. I had the opportunity to visit shut-ins at Immaculate Heart of Mary and saw many who had been parishioners 40 years earlier. I enjoyed spending time with Father Ruffolo who had also spent a good portion of his life as pastor of that church.

The Sunday Liturgies there are invigorating. The parish

marimba ensemble provides music at the main Masses, and as the crowds pour out into the street after Mass they are greeted by vendors in a setting reminiscent of old Mexico, offering a variety of *antojitos* from *churros* to *enchiladas suizas*. The parish is a center for continuous activity that is evident throughout the week. Close to 1,000 children receive religious instruction from well-trained volunteers. *Padres Ayudando a Padres* (Parents Helping Parents) is a program through which families help one another in the training of their children. Sadly there is still an element of violence in the neighborhood.

One Saturday morning while brushing my teeth, I heard a staccato sound, which I recognized as gunshots. My arthritic legs gradually brought me down the two flights of stairs in the rectory and onto the street. There I recognized the figure of Father Bruce bent over the body of a young person who moments before had been shot by someone in a passing car—a scene too often repeated in a very overcrowded neighborhood. Struggling to destroy this culture of death and replace it with a life-giving *raison d'etre* is a challenge to the Claretians as they live and work in the inner city of this great metropolis.

> *St. Anthony Claret gathered those who had lost their faith.... Instead of fibers and threads, he wove the fabric of people's lives. He created the cloth of dignity, peace, and faith, always using the most "common threads."* —Common Threads, The Life and Spirit of St. Anthony Claret

Now I am back at Corpus Chrisii in Stone Mountain, enjoying a very active retirement. At one time the parish had about 3,500 families, mainly transferees to the South from the Northeast and Midwest for employment or retirement, but the number has presently decreased due to a few societal shifts in the population. Many white residents in the area have moved to cities, subdivisions, and parishes outside of Stone Mountain, referring to their exodus as "white flight."

The parish had also suffered greatly because of two pedophilia cases in 1985 and again in 1987. The alleged clergy offenders have been disciplined and incarcerated, but the parishioners felt abandoned and this was in no way alleviated when they heard that a "missionary" order would be administering their parish. The parishioners were not given any information about our order before we arrived, but it was not long before the Claretians began to work in perfect harmony with the existing staff and 40 lay ministries within the parish. Presently, the faith community numbers approximately 1,500 families and represents many different ethnic cultures including Caucasian, Hispanic, European, Black, Caribbean, American, Indian, Nigerian, and Filipino. Much has been done to refurbish the worship center and the entire physical plant. Since 1992, 12 Claretian priests have ministered at this parish, their transfers being due to either sickness or their talents required elsewhere. Father Greg Kenny and I are the only two left of the original four "founding" Claretians.

During my ministry in Stone Mountain, I have been most impressed by the spirit of family that exists among the parishioners. Corpus Christi has been—and is—a eucharistic community. In 1997 a perpetual adoration chapel was established, and since then the eucharistic presence has had company, 24 hours a day, 365 days of the year. Parishioners are drawn not only to the eucharistic presence but also Christ's presence in the community. It recognizes the dignity of each member regardless of color or ethnic background. This community reaches out to all in need and warms up to all who join together in worship. Pride reigns for many parishioners who call Corpus Christi "my family, my house, my church."

This recognition of Christ in the poor and abandoned has prompted the parish to adopt a mission run by Father Ho Lung in Kingston, Jamaica. At various times throughout the year several of our parishioners, through a ministry called Missionaries of the Poor, spend a week at this site to attend the sick, help with the daily routine, and provide necessary items—all under the leadership of our pastoral assistant, Gini Eagen.

Also at Corpus Christi, the St. Vincent de Paul Society established a thrift store for donations of clothing and household items that are collected, often refurbished, and then sold at a minimum cost to families in need. Along with the store, volunteer workers collect and distribute a sum exceeding $80,000 annually to the poor—this amount coming from the monthly contributions of the faithful who attend Sunday worship and donate specifically to this fund.

Some have been predicting the demise of this parish because of demographics, but so far it has been an exciting and productive place, and we will continue in our efforts to keep it as healthy as it has been.

Conclusion

Through these pages I have taken you on the journey of my life. As we skimmed the waves of time, we paused at various locations of my life in the priesthood. This year, 2004, marks the 50th anniversary of the Claretian Eastern province, and the 60th anniversary of my ordination to the priesthood. As such, I decided to acquaint you with the many places served by the Claretian Missionaries, and to illustrate all that our order is doing to bring God's love into our apostolic centers.

In the narration of my life, from its nadir to its zenith, I have mentioned some interruptions or challenges I have referred to as el poche syndrome, a phenomenon that perhaps others might have experienced at critical moments of their lives and simply ignored as a temporary psychological aberration.

As I mature in my priesthood and look back at my inner struggles, I find a logical explanation to which I refer when identifying my turning point: God's grace! Ordination to the priesthood is a conferring of a sacrament. Upon being ordained I received the grace of that sacrament, and through this grace I was configured with Christ in his role as a shepherd, and as head of the church. The grace of ordination allows me to act in the person of Christ, and this should transform me and establish my identity.

Perhaps I gradually strayed away from this truth. I attempted to be a good priest, but in the process I may have confused being a good priest with being a successful priest. The trinitarian love that gave birth to creation and prompted the Son of God to be born in a manger is the same love that led him to accept the cross, is the same compassionate love that Christ as a shepherd now calls others to share and spread throughout the world.

St. Anthony Claret, in describing a Claretian, writes:

A Claretian is a person on fire with the love of God who desires to spread it wherever he goes. Nothing daunts him, he delights in privation, he welcomes work, embraces sacrifices, smiles at slander, and rejoices in suffering. His only concern is how to best follow Christ and imitate him.

These words have encouraged me to tell my story. As I celebrate and thank God for 86 years of life, 60 of those years in the priesthood, I ask as you read these memoirs to join me in thanking God for the compassionate love he gave to me—El Poche!

Acknowledgments:

Many thanks to Dottie Lauer, secretary of Corpus Christi Parish in Stone Mountain, Georgia, for her typing and preparation of the manuscript, as well as to Tara Dix at Claretian Publications in Chicago, who made the final edits to the book.

The purchase of this book will benefit the Claretian mission of Tierra Nueva in Juarez, Chihuahua, Mexico.